ANY
WEDNESDAY

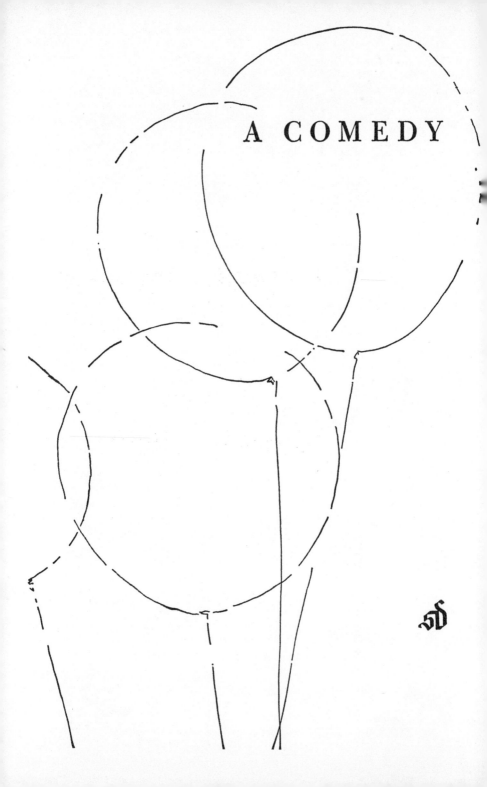

A COMEDY

BY *Muriel Resnik*

ANY
WEDNESDAY

STEIN AND DAY/*Publishers*/New York

Published simultaneously in Canada
by S. J. Reginald Saunders & Co., Ltd.

Designed by David Miller.

Photos by Wallace Litwin.

Printed in the United States of America.

ANY WEDNESDAY

Premiere Performance, February 18, 1964

at the Music Box Theater

PRODUCERS:

George W. George & Frank Granat
Howard Erskine, Edward Specter Productions, Peter S. Katz

THE CAST:

ELLEN ——————————————————————————— Sandy Dennis
JOHN ———————————————————————————— Don Porter
DOROTHY ————————————————————————— Rosemary Murphy
CASS ———————————————————————————— Gene Hackman

Directed by Henry Kaplan
Scenery designed by Robert Randolph
Lighting by Tharon Musser
Costumes by Theoni V. Aldredge
Hair styles by Kenneth

ANY
WEDNESDAY

THE CAST:

JOHN
ELLEN
CASS
DOROTHY

THE SETTING:

A garden apartment in the
East Sixties, Manhattan

ACT ONE

Scene 1: Thursday noon in July
Scene 2: That evening, 7:30

ACT TWO

Scene 1: Later the same evening
Scene 2: Thursday noon a week later

ACT ONE

Scene 1

PLACE: *A garden apartment in the East Sixties, Manhattan.
The living room is light, gay, charming, and comfortable
though some of the furniture is bizarre Victorian and some
merely bizarre. The general effect is a happy clutter. There is
a desk, a small sofa with a coffee table before it, an old apothe-
cary chest of drawers, an antique French telephone with an
overly long cord, a Victorian display easel, a busy bulletin
board, and a large, ornate, church candlestick. The walls are
strewn with paintings, prints, framed trivia, and various sou-
venirs of travel. Through windows and a door, stage right, a
terrace and garden are visible. Beneath the windows, a window seat masks a radiator. The entrance door is center stage
rear beside a closet door hung with a Victorian mirror. Left
stage are the door to the bedroom and the swinging door to
the kitchen. A lawnmower is propped in an unobtrusive corner,*

11

the floor around the desk is littered with long strips of galley proofs, and near the kitchen a small table is set for breakfast for two.

TIME: *A Thursday noon in July.*

AT RISE: JOHN *enters from the bedroom, jaunty and freshly showered. He is a lean, elegant man in his late forties or early fifties, vital, dynamic, accustomed to having his own way, wearing the aura of success as naturally as his Cartier links and Peale shoes. He crosses to the front door, opens it, and picks up* The New York Times *from the hall floor. He closes the door, scanning the headlines.*

JOHN (*Calling*). Darling! I'm out of the shower. (*Crosses to the table and seats himself.*)

ELLEN (*Off*). Coming.

(ELLEN *enters from the kitchen carrying a coffee pot. She is young, lovely, vulnerable, her face at once bright, eager, and wistful. She wears an extravagant, dramatic, completely impractical negligée, its yards of skirt floating and billowing as she walks, the sleeves ballooning and drooping over her wrists and hands. She is preoccupied, her smile an afterthought.*)

JOHN. You didn't remember to call the man about the air conditioner.

ELLEN (*Pouring coffee*). Yes I did. He can't come until Monday.

JOHN. Monday! But this is only Thursday!

ELLEN. John, I promise you it will be fixed before next Wednesday. (*Noticing headline on* JOHN's *newspaper.*)

Russia *still* hasn't paid her dues. I think I'll picket the U.N. today.

JOHN. That's the way I like to think of you—with a sign around your neck . . . (*As* ELLEN *sits,* JOHN *gives her the second section of the paper.*) Can't you do anything with those sleeves?

ELLEN (*Opening paper*). No. They're supposed to be like this. You said you bought it because the sleeves were so graceful.

JOHN. Next time I'll get you something with long, tight ones or none at all.

ELLEN. I think it's beautiful.

JOHN. That's just because you're in it.

ELLEN (*Studying paper*). Oh, here's a picture of your wife. "Mrs. John Cleves, Chairman of the April in Paris Ball, lunching at Pavillon."

JOHN (*Uncomfortably*). Dorothy's very busy with good works, too. (*Referring to his paper.*) There they go again—bottling the tax bill in committee. They kill it every time because it might conceivably help the rich.

ELLEN (*Sympathetic, putting her paper aside*). It's so unfair, John, that out of every ten dollars you make, you have to give back nine.

JOHN. Nine-twenty—

ELLEN. But it really gets to be terrible when you make a hundred thousand and you have to give back ninety thousand —ninety-two thousand—

JOHN. Sweetheart, I've told you that it doesn't work *quite* that way. We of the underprivileged do what we can wherever we can.

ELLEN (*Bright and sweet*). Yes, you do. You do that. Yes indeedy. Wherever you can. That's right, all right.

JOHN. What's the matter?

ELLEN. Oh, nothing. . . . My usual morning thoughts . . . about how I loathe being tax-deductible.

JOHN. I've told you thousands of times, Ellen, this apartment is *yours.*

ELLEN. Not any more, it's not. It *was,* before I even *met* you, but when it went co-op you bought it in the name of the *company* for their *executive suite.*

JOHN. You know it's never been used for that—that's nothing but a tax dodge! Ellen, I'm surprised at you. A girl with your public spirit! This is what the Internal Revenue Service expects. It's all part of the game. They play their part, we have to play ours. It's our duty as American citizens!

ELLEN. I don't care. It makes me feel as if I were an IBM machine!

JOHN. Sweetheart, what's wrong? What's *really* bothering you? Come on . . . you can tell me.

ELLEN (*A beat*). It's my birthday.

JOHN (*Putting her on*). No! Slipped my mind completely! . . . Put your hand in my pocket . . . No, the other one.

(ELLEN *draws out a diamond necklace and holds it up, stunned.*) Happy birthday, pet. You said once that you

14

thought a diamond necklace was an insanely foolish luxury . . . Well, I've always thought every pretty girl should have *something* foolish. . . .

ELLEN. Oh, John . . . I didn't expect anything . . . I didn't want you to . . .

JOHN (*Putting necklace around her neck*). Here. Let me see how you look all dressed up.

ELLEN. I'm so . . . so touched. . . .

JOHN. It's exactly right for you. I knew it would be.

ELLEN. How could you go wrong?

JOHN. Well-l-l . . . it was a little tricky. Cartier designed it especially for us . . . rather ingenious the way they worked in the Blo-Cold trademark. You don't really see it unless you're looking for it . . . Oh pet, you'll have to let the agency use it whenever they do another Blo-Cold Refrigerator ad, but—

ELLEN (*Crosses to mirror, stares at herself, patting necklace as if it were an infant*). I'll never take it off . . . when I have it—not for the rest of my life. (*Crossing to* JOHN.) If the agency can spare it, I'll be . . . buried in it.

JOHN. What a thing to say! You're still a child!

ELLEN. I'm not! I'm—John, you just can't understand—it's so horrible to be—oh God—*thirty*. . . .

JOHN (*Takes her in his arms*). Pet, you're still in kindergarten. Look at me! I'm . . . whatever I am . . . and I still think of myself as twenty-two.

ELLEN. It's different for a woman! Today is a turning point in my life, the beginning of the end. It's pushing forty—and menopause out there waiting to spring—and before you can even turn around you're a senior citizen.

JOHN. Ellen, you don't look a day over twelve—

ELLEN. —Oh, what a silly thing to say!

JOHN. —Sixteen then—

ELLEN. —Oh—

JOHN. —Eighteen! And you and I will be eighteen and twenty-two forever.

ELLEN (*Wan*). You're sweet, John.

JOHN. I've got another present for you.

ELLEN. (*Again a child playing a game*). Where is it?

JOHN. Right here.

ELLEN. Where? I don't see anything—

JOHN. It's me. For the day.

ELLEN (*Sinks to sofa*). I can't believe it.

JOHN (*Sitting beside her*). It took a little doing. I told the office that as far as anyone is concerned I'm still out of town. As far as *they're* concerned, I'm spending the day at the executive suite, working. So, my love, I have an absolutely free day, all clear, and I give it to you.

ELLEN. Oh, John, that's the best present I've ever had! It's the sweetest, nicest thing anyone's ever done for me. Oh John, I love you *so*. A whole day! We've never had a day together, only pieces of Wednesdays.

JOHN. I thought you'd be pleased. Now, it's your day, what would you like to do with it?

ELLEN. We can be like people—like anybody—we won't have to stay locked up here— Oh, I'm so excited I can't stand it! Let's go to Coney Island and ride a roller coaster.

JOHN (*A pause*). . . . It's your day, what would you like to do with it?

ELLEN. You don't like Coney Island.

JOHN. The last time I was on a roller coaster I couldn't wait to get off. Almost jumped the second time around.

ELLEN (*Sympathetic*). Ohhh . . . I know! Let's go to the Modern Museum and see the new exhibit.

JOHN. That's a little touchy, sweetheart. I'm on the Board of Directors, and they know me there.

ELLEN. That's all right. Then we'll go to the Metropolitan . . . They know you there . . . You know what would be fun? Could we have lunch on the terrace in the Central Park Zoo?

JOHN. Angel. . . .

ELLEN. You're a director of the Zoo?

JOHN. It's not only that . . . I'm recognized. Wherever I go now all sorts of people come up and ask me to autograph money for them . . . ever since that piece in *Time* magazine—

ELLEN (*Reciting*). "Publicity-shy John Cleves is a slim, handsome man with the ruthlessness of an eagle." Did I get it right?

JOHN. Not quite, sweetheart. It's "the *expertise* and ruthless-ness of an eagle." —And I wish they'd never printed it.

ELLEN (*Warm and reassuring*). We can stay right here. It doesn't matter what we do as long as we're together. That's the real present! Do you know it started out to be the worst day of my life and now it's the best? Oh John, you're the most marvelous lover a lady ever had. . . .

JOHN. I'm the last of the great ones. You didn't know that, did you, you lucky girl.

ELLEN. I know. . . . You keep telling me.

JOHN. And to commemorate the occasion I'm buying myself a little present.

(*Crosses to phone, dials.*)

Sweet Sam, only the greatest stallion in the history of horse racing! And a steal at $850,000. I want to check with Pete Mitchell. I'm changing his name to Ellen.

ELLEN. You can't call a stallion Ellen.

JOHN. A rose by any other name—Pete? What about the horse? What do you mean you hear they're bidding a million! Don't you know? . . . There are ways of finding out! I pay you for facts not rumors! Pete, I want that horse! Get him! (*Slams down phone.*)

ELLEN. What does all that mean?

JOHN. It means Sam may never become Ellen. And I've got a hundred brood mares in Kentucky waiting for that old boy! But we're not going to let that spoil our day, are we? You think about what you'd like to do while I make one

18

more call, the last one. (*Dials.*) I have to check with the office. I don't trust that new secretary.

ELLEN (*Inspired*). I know! If you'd sit for me I'd paint your portrait. I've always wanted to, and there's never been time —I'd sketch you in oils—like a drawing—and I'd give it to you so if you don't get Sam you'd still have something—

JOHN. It wouldn't mean much to the mares, but I'd treasure it. What the hell's wrong with the switchboard? They're all Radcliffe girls with genius I.Q.'s, can't even find a hole—

(ELLEN *takes paint box from corner, sets it on chair, opens it.*)

Hello? This is Mr. Cleves. Will you tell Miss Linsley—I don't want to speak to her—

ELLEN (*Exiting to kitchen*). —And we'll have a picnic in the garden—

JOHN (*Pacing, getting tangled in cord*). Miss Linsley? No, I'm not in Cleveland. I'm not at the airport. Miss Linsley—I'm at the executive suite— Late for what appointment? I told you to make *no* appointments for today, this is Thursday! Oh my God! Not *next* Thursday, I said *this* Thursday, *today!* How *could* you have misunderstood? Tell him to come back tomorrow— Leaving for Saudi Arabia? . . . Oh God, lunch with the British Ambassador—the Attorney General —Mrs. Cleves' theater tickets? Call Mrs. Cleves at once— She's already left Short Hills? Miss Linsley, will you do something for me? Will you just clasp your hands on your desk and *don't move* until I get there? (*Slams phone down.*)

ELLEN (*Enters*). We're going to have egg salad on pumpernickel for lunch—

JOHN. Sweetheart—

ELLEN (*Testing brushes and palette*). It's going to be such a lovely day.

JOHN. Sweetheart, that monster has made an appointment for me this morning, man from Saudi Arabia who's flying back this afternoon. He's waiting in my office now.

ELLEN. Ohhh. . . . Well, that's all right.

(*Closes paint box.*)

You hurry up and see him, and I'll clean the house and fix lunch for us—

JOHN. It seems that I'm lunching with the British Ambassador before he leaves for London.

ELLEN (*Brave and managing a smile*). We'll still have the whole afternoon—

JOHN. Miss Linsley should be shot, and I may do it myself. After lunch I have two other appointments before the Mayor's Cultural Committee meets at my office.

ELLEN (*Crushed*). . . . That's the whole day.

JOHN. Why don't you take your friend Janice to lunch—

ELLEN. Janice is in Easthampton and Corky's back with the circus and Nancy's pregnant.

JOHN. How about a movie? The other night Dorothy and I— (*Catches himself.*)

ELLEN. I thought you never went to the movies.

JOHN. Once in a great while.

ELLEN (*Replaces paint box in corner*). If you haven't seen it, you should really try to see *Divorce Italian Style*. It's about this man who can't get a divorce so he murders his wife.

JOHN. Ellen, don't! . . . I'm just as disappointed as you—

ELLEN. I know you are. I love you, John. It was such a beautiful thought. Let's try again next year . . . (*Happy again.*) And we still have tonight! We forgot about that! We've never had two nights in a row—

JOHN. Angel—

ELLEN. As I was saying, we've never had two nights in a row—

JOHN. If it were anything else . . . but, thanks to Miss Linsley, Dorothy has theater tickets for tonight . . .

ELLEN. Oh, that's all right. . . . (*Sweet and interested.*) How is Dorothy?

JOHN. She's fine.

ELLEN. And Johnny?

JOHN. He's fine, too.

TOGETHER. Debby?

JOHN. They're all fine.

ELLEN. Good. I hope you get Sweet Sam. (*Crossing to door.*)

JOHN. I'll get him. I always get what I want.

ELLEN. Yes, you do, darling.

JOHN. I don't have to tell you how I feel about our beautiful day. (*Takes briefcase and crosses to her.*)

ELLEN. Maybe someday we'll have one. . . .

JOHN. I hate to think of you alone here. . . .

ELLEN. I'm not alone. I have all the things I love . . . my garden, my funny chair . . . and you are always with me . . .
oh dear, I'm getting corny . . . See you next Wednesday.
(*Opens door.*)

JOHN. I'll kill Miss Linsley with my bare hands. Try to have
a nice day. And remember the necklace is yours, this apartment is yours, and you don't look a day over twelve. Call
you when I get to the office.

(JOHN *kisses* ELLEN *and exits. She watches him down the hall
for a moment, then closes the door, turns to the mirror and
briefly studies herself for signs of age, gazes at the necklace
with complete disinterest, then around the empty room and
sighs, bereft and forlorn. She crosses to the table, picks up
some cups and plates, trails to the kitchen door, then suddenly
throws them through the door to shatter on the kitchen floor,
whips the cloth off the table with the glasses, toast rack, etc.
and exits into the kitchen. In a moment she enters carrying a
small iced cake with a large candle stuck in it. Wading through
the debris she crosses to the sofa, seats herself, carefully ar-
ranging yards of skirt, and lights the candle. Gazing into the
flame she makes a solemn wish, then blows it out. Her hand
wanders unconsciously to the necklace. She takes it off, studies
it, and filled with rage, buries it under the pillows and collapses
upon them sobbing, howling, and beating them with her fists.*
    The door opens and CASS *lets himself in with a key. A large
man in his late thirties with the look of the unaccustomed
visitor to Manhattan, his features are rugged, overlaid with
humor. He carries a raincoat and a suitcase. He sees* ELLEN,
*surveys the mess on the floor, and looks uncertainly at the key
in his hand, goes back to check the number on the outside of*

the door to be sure that he's in the right place, decides that he is, closes the door, sets the suitcase and coat on the floor, and crosses to ELLEN. *For a moment he studies her thrashing body with appreciation mingled with compassion, then he kneels beside her, touches her shoulder gently.*)

CASS. Come on now, honey. Take a deep breath, and pull yourself together.

ELLEN (*Screams, leaps to her feet in panic*). Who *are* you?

CASS. Poor kid. Had a rough night, didn't you?

(ELLEN *rushes to phone.*)

Hey, hey, hey—I'm not going to hurt you.

ELLEN. *Who are you?*

CASS. I didn't break and enter. (*Shows key.*) It's okay! My name's Cass Henderson and Miss Linsley said—

ELLEN. Miss Linsley?—

CASS. The one with all the teeth. She said it would be all right; with the convention in town and all I'd never get a hotel room, and she knew Mr. Cleves would want me to be comfortable—

ELLEN. Mr. Henderson, I'm sure the company is eager to accommodate you—

CASS. Accommodate? . . . (*With an attempt at worldliness.*) That's all right, honey, I know you have to say that, but I didn't get much sleep last night. . . . Oh, no offense! I think you're beautiful! Gee, they've got an air conditioner, why don't you turn it on? (*Starts for machine.*) Make you feel better.

23

ELLEN. It's broken.

CASS. They broke the air conditioner, too? Some party!

ELLEN (*Puts phone down*). Mr. Henderson!

CASS. You putting your little brother through school or something?

(ELLEN *whimpers.*)

Gee, you're kind of emotional for this business. Everybody has to make a living, but a girl like you, young and strong, you could do anything—salesgirl, receptionist, file clerk—

ELLEN. Mister Henderson, you have got to get *out* of here. This . . . is my . . . I *live* here . . . You're invading the privacy of my *home*.

CASS. I thought it was the executive suite.

ELLEN. It is the executive suite.

CASS. Oh.

ELLEN. But it isn't.

CASS. I see . . . Miss Linsley said it was the executive—

ELLEN. Miss Linsley is new. She thinks it *is* the executive suite. She doesn't know it *isn't*.

CASS. But if you live here . . . and this is company property . . . What are you doing living on company property?

ELLEN. . . . It's a special arrangement . . . like a scholarship.

CASS. Oh, a grant, like the Ford Foundation?

ELLEN. More like a Fullbright. (*Crossing to door.*) Now will you please go?

24

CASS (*Moving to his bag*). Okay . . . okay . . .

ELLEN. Please hurry! I want to get out of these sleeves and clean up this mess.

CASS. All right . . . I'm going . . . But would you mind if I use your phone? Just to call a buddy of mine and see if he'll take me in?

ELLEN (*Dubious*). If you must.

CASS. Thanks.

ELLEN. Must you?

CASS (*On his way to phone*). Thanks a lot. Go ahead and get out of your sleeves. I can let myself out. Go ahead. I won't take anything.

ELLEN (*Grudgingly*). Well, you'd better be gone when I come out. (*Opens bedroom door, starts inside, turns back, unenthusiastically.*) Nice meeting you. (*Exits, slamming door.*)

CASS (*As* ELLEN *exits*). My pleasure, Miss—uh— (*Dials.*) Operator give me Akron, Ohio, collect to 253-2311. The area code is 216. Cass Henderson calling. This number is (*Peering at phone.*) RE 4-7098. (*Waits, whistling, looking around the room.*) Betty? Fine. Put me right on to my brother, will you, hon? I can't hang on this phone. (*Blows kiss into phone.*) George? You know where I am? I'm phoning you from the executive suite of Cleves, Inc. Never mind how, George. God is on our side. No, Cleves isn't here, but somebody else is . . . A girl . . . She lives here on a special arrangement . . . Getting out of her sleeves . . . *Sleeves.* . . . Please, will you just shut up and listen? She says it's like

25

a scholarship . . . Well, you know what that means, somebody's keeping her, right? So if I can hang around maybe I can find out who—must be somebody big in the company. Maybe she even knows Cleves himself, who knows? . . . But it's worth a try. . . . It's last chance, desperation time. We haven't been able to get to the bastard any other way.

(ELLEN *enters from bedroom, barefoot, dressed in blue jeans and a man's shirt. She stands, hands on hips, glaring at Cass.*)

Yeah, but you're the fourth old pal I've called, old pal. Sure, I understand. Let's get together for a drink. (*Hangs up.*)

ELLEN. OUT!!

CASS. Miss Linsley was right. The hotels are booked solid, and nobody in New York has a guest room.

ELLEN. Mr. Henderson, why don't you go away?

CASS. I'm going . . . but one of the guys is calling me back here— You'll let me stay long enough to get that call, won't you?

ELLEN (*A pause*). Are you a guest of Cleves, Inc.? Or what are you?

CASS. Henderson Machine and Tool. Cleves took us over six months ago.

ELLEN. Are you sure your friend is going to call?

CASS. His secretary said he just stepped out of the office for a minute.

ELLEN. Mr. Henderson, I'm expecting a call myself and I'd like a little privacy. Couldn't you go somewhere and call your friend back? There's a sweet little booth at the end of the block with big windows.

CASS. Now look, Miss . . . uh . . . Why don't you sit down and read a magazine or something, have a cup of coffee . . . (*Picking up dishes and placing them on table.*) . . . and I'll clean up this mess while I'm waiting.

ELLEN (*Sweeping them off the table*). I'll clean up my own mess, thank you.

CASS (*Putting more dishes on table*). That's not nice, honey.

(ELLEN *sweeps them off.*)

I *said* that's not nice.

ELLEN. I'll scream!

(*Screams. As* ELLEN *screams, the door opens and we see* DOROTHY CLEVES. *She is fortyish and unmistakably a lady, slim, chic, and most attractive, dressed very simply in an elderly Mainbocher, nonetheless elegant for the passage of years. She surveys the scene and checks door number.* ELLEN *turns to follow* CASS's *gaze.*)

DOROTHY (*Obviously the product of a finishing school*). How do you do. I'm Dorothy Cleves.

CASS. How do you do. I'm Cass Henderson. And this is . . .

DOROTHY. I'm so sorry I've disturbed you. I didn't know—Miss Linsley didn't mention— (ELLEN *turns to* CASS *and sags into his arms.*)

DOROTHY (*Tactfully, as she hurries to help*). We all get a little weak in the knees in this weather. (*As* CASS *props* ELLEN *on a dining chair* DOROTHY *immediately pulls* ELLEN's

27

legs apart and pushes her head down between her knees.)
Shouldn't we get your wife a glass of water?

(CASS *makes a false start into the wrong door, quickly corrects himself and exits into kitchen.*)

I've never been here— (*Fanning, massaging back of* ELLEN's *neck.*) It belongs to my husband's company—the executive suite—but of course you know that. (*Pulls* ELLEN *up into sitting position.*) You come to New York often? (*Fanning* ELLEN *with her glove as* CASS *enters with water, takes glass from him, holds it to* ELLEN's *mouth.*)

CASS. Sort of—

DOROTHY (*Fanning* ELLEN). Where do you usually stay?

CASS. . . . We . . .

DOROTHY. I prefer the St. Regis myself, though I don't think it's quite the same since Vincent passed on— Oh, but you stay here, don't you? After all, that's what it's for. Is there no air conditioning?

CASS. It seems to be broken.

DOROTHY. Dreadful. Well, at least the theaters are cool and the Aquarium is *charming.* I suppose you're wondering why I'm here . . . as well you might—I wanted to catch John before he left . . .

(ELLEN *slowly flops over.* DOROTHY *pulls her up, gives glass of water back to* ELLEN *who sips sullenly.*)

Just keep sipping, dear. (*To* CASS.) You saw my husband, didn't you. I must have just missed him, I was at Maximilian's first thing this morning—you see, last week I came into town to shop—it must have been Wednesday because

28

John was in Chicago—no, he was in Chicago yesterday . . .
or was yesterday Cleveland . . . oh well, it was last week
that I saw the coat at Maximilian and I haven't been able
to sleep since. I've *never* coveted anything in my life the
way I— (*Now wandering around room.*) —*adore* church
candlesticks. *Such* a sense of history . . . I dashed back
there this morning and they reduced it for me. (*Crosses to
coffee table.*) Floribundas and heliotrope . . . now that's
charming. More than I can say about the rest of the place
—Took the price down more than half! I suppose because
it's July, you know, but it's the most incredible buy! And
there's nothing more practical than sable—it's so all-purpose
—I left a deposit and dashed to the office to fetch John
before they changed their minds and he wasn't there of
course, but his new secretary, Miss Linsley—I've always felt
orthodontia at the right time is worth every penny, don't
you? Miss Linsley told me he stopped off here. (*Wandering around the room.*) Do you know I hadn't the slightest
notion there *was* an executive suite? But that's John, so
much on his mind. So I dashed up, and here I am and I
must admit, *thoroughly appalled.* Overdone, diffuse, bizarre, obviously done by someone insecure. Probably cost
a fortune, too. I could have done so much with— (*Stopped
by mess on floor.*) Can't *imagine* when it was last cleaned!
I *must* apologize. I'm sure it's tax-deductible, but so is a
cleaning woman—

(ELLEN *flops over,* DOROTHY *runs to her and pulls her up.*)

Coffee might help.

(CASS *looks in pot, takes it and exits to kitchen.*)

Feeling any better? Your color seems to have come back

a bit. (*Takes glasses out of purse, puts them on.*) I'll never get used to these . . . Bifocals. Tried contact lenses, but John found the glint in my eye too disturbing—he can't *abide* change. Yes, you do seem to be rallying—it's this ghastly weather.

CASS (*Enters from kitchen with champagne bottle*). I couldn't find any coffee. Isn't this a kind of a stimulant?

DOROTHY. Champagne! How charming!

(CASS *uncorks bottle.*)

Adore that sound. Makes me think of midnight sailings . . . so festive . . .

(ELLEN *grabs bottle from* CASS *and tips it to her lips.*)

CASS. She's got a real thing about champagne, just can't get enough of it. How about I get some glasses, dear, and Mrs. Cleves can join us—(*He exits to kitchen.*)

DOROTHY. How nice! A party! A surprise party!

(CASS *re-enters with a tray and three glasses, gently takes bottle from* ELLEN *and pours.*)

Yes, whenever we went to Europe we launched ourselves with magnums of champagne; but it's been years since I've been anywhere, bound to the hearth. John *loathes* traveling—goes off Wednesdays, *collapses* Thursdays—

(*When two glasses have been filled,* ELLEN *grabs bottle.* CASS *takes* DOROTHY'S *glass to her. The phone rings.* CASS *is the closest to it.*)

CASS. Hello? Hello? (*Hangs up.*)

ELLEN (*Huskily*). Wrong number?

CASS. No voice. Just heavy breathing. Some kind of a nut.

DOROTHY (*Toasting*). To the Hendersons.

CASS. To our host and hostess—

(*The phone rings.* ELLEN, *bottle still in hand manages to get to it first.*)

ELLEN. Hello? No. No one. No I can't imagine who it could have been . . . (*Nervous glance at* CASS *and* DOROTHY.) Oh, silly . . . (*Very brightly.*) Listen Giselle, I was just about to step into the tub. Call you back, huh? (*Hangs up.*)

DOROTHY. You are feeling better . . .

ELLEN. Oh, I'm just dandy. (*Swigs from bottle.*)

CASS (*Reaches for the bottle*). Sweetheart . . .

(ELLEN *turns away from him, clutching the champagne to her bosom.*)

DOROTHY. I must run along. Don't want to keep you from your bath, Mrs. Henderson—

CASS. Oh, don't go.

(ELLEN *tugs at back of* CASS's *jacket.*)

DOROTHY. I really should. I have so much to do. (*Touches arm of sofa disapprovingly.*) It's been wonderful meeting you, so young, your lives stretching before you— Do you have children?

CASS. Uh—

ELLEN. Not yet.

DOROTHY. You're just a child yourself.

ELLEN. I've aged today. (*Catches herself.*) It's my birthday.
(*Indicates cake.*)

DOROTHY (*Stricken*). Well! Happy birthday! . . . I want to tell
you something, both of you, something told to me by a very
wise woman on my wedding day. It's my birthday present
to you, my dear, and believe me, it works—John and I
have been married for years you know—Dorothy, she said,
never, never, *never* go to sleep angry at each other. And
do you know, whatever discord John and I may have had
during the day, oh *little* things, we have *never*—
(*Phone rings,* ELLEN *grabs it.*)

ELLEN. Hello.

DOROTHY (*To* CASS). —And we have an *immoderately* happy
marriage.

ELLEN (*Biting each word*). Giselle, I told you I was getting
into the tub. No, I'm not in it yet, of course I'm not, how
can I be when you keep calling? I told you I'd call you
back! (*Slams phone down.*)

DOROTHY. I must really go and beard the lion in his lair. But
before I do I want to see you kids kiss and make up and
no more nonsense. Just to please me? (*Pushes* CASS *toward*
ELLEN.)

CASS (*Crosses to* ELLEN). Darling?
(ELLEN *walks away.*)

She didn't understand. (*Following her.*) Honeybun, I
know Mrs. Cleves said never to go to bed without . . . uh
. . . and I know just what you're thinking. Oh yes I do. That

we just got out of bed. But . . . (*Pulls* ELLEN *down on his knee. She struggles to get away as* DOROTHY *peers politely at paintings.*) . . . let's be friends.

DOROTHY (*Turning to them*). There. Now I feel much better.

ELLEN. I'm glad.

DOROTHY. Don't you?

ELLEN. No.

DOROTHY. Sometimes it takes a little effort to make the emotional adjustment from anger to love, although psychologically speaking, they're so closely akin—

CASS. I'm feeling better every minute.

DOROTHY. Of course you are. Now I'll leave you two to adjust to each other. But before I go, do you mind if I take a quick look at the garden? (*Crossing to garden door.*) Is that grass?

(ELLEN *struggles to get away from* CASS.)

I can't *imagine* anyone foolish enough to try a lawn in this city. Flagstone's the only thing. I'll bring my own man along. My word! Those hideous lavender flowers—

(ELLEN *breaks free and stands.*)

It *can't* be wisteria blooming in July—I should never drink champagne in the morning.

(DOROTHY *turns to see* CASS *trying to get* ELLEN *back on his lap, bites her lip, then*)

I've just had the most *brilliant* idea! John and I shall take you to dinner tonight! Our treat—

ELLEN (*As she quickly sits on* CASS's *knee, patting his cheek*).
No, no, Mrs. Cleves, you mustn't change your plans for us.

DOROTHY. We have no plans at all, just killing an evening in
town—

ELLEN. Your theater tickets—

DOROTHY. Miss Linsley'll call the broker and cancel them. Or
use them herself. Now that's settled. We'll pick you up
here at eight. Pavillon, hum? It's quiet enough so that we
can all get to know each other better . . . And then we'll
do the town a bit. New York can be *very* jolly off season.
Now just try not to be aware of your environment. The next
time you come to stay it'll be quite, quite different.
(*Crosses to door, taking last look around room, turns to*
ELLEN.) Mrs. Henderson, how did you know we had theater tickets? I don't remember mentioning it. . . .

ELLEN (*After a beat*). Didn't you?

DOROTHY (*Bemused*). Perhaps I did. Eight o'clock. Good-by.

(*Exits smiling, closes door.*)

(ELLEN *remains on* CASS's *knee, in shock.*)

CASS. Are you all right? Hey, how *did* you know they had
theater tickets? She didn't mention it. So how did you know
they were going to the theater? . . . Dear?

ELLEN (*Jumps to her feet*). Will you get out of here?

CASS. Honey, we just kissed and made up. Remember, I'm
your husband. (*Phone rings.* CASS *is nearer.*) Hello? Hello?
(*Looking at dial.*) Yes, this is RE 4-7098. Just a minute.
Would there be a Miss Gordon around here anywhere?

(ELLEN *grabs the phone.*)

Oh! How do you do!

ELLEN. Hello? Well yes, I'll tell you all about it, but not now
. . . The whole morning's been very weird. . . . All sorts of
strange things. . . . Well, you know Miss Linsley? Mr.
Cleves' secretary? She sent him here because she said he
probably couldn't get a room in a hotel. Someone should
have a sharp word with her. I've got one *for* her—Hello?
(*Hangs up.*)

CASS. So how long *have* you been living here?

ELLEN. *Must I have you removed by force?*

CASS. As soon as I get my call—

ELLEN (*Pacing*). Are you *sure* your friend's going to call?

CASS (*Waving away her doubts*). He'll call—

ELLEN. What are you going to do about that dinner tonight?

CASS. Go. But you don't have to if you don't want to. (*Phone
rings.*) There he is now. (*Crosses to phone.*) Hello? Hi,
Giselle, how are you? (*Hands phone to* ELLEN, *crosses to
sofa, stretches out.*)

ELLEN (*Into phone*). Well you didn't let me *finish*—he's waiting for a call, that's all. You *did* speak to Miss Linsley?
Then she told you. I mean, did she tell you *everything*?
No, no, we haven't been alone. Oh, didn't Miss Linsley tell
you? Mrs. Cleves stopped at the office and Miss Linsley
sent *her* up here too—hello? (*Hangs up.*)

CASS. Mrs. Cleves is a nice lady.

35

ELLEN. Oh? Did you think so? (*Mounting fury.*) Well, she'd better keep her wretched, itchy fingers off this place. (*Pacing.*) It's mine. Filthy, unoriginal, uncharming, diffuse, *bizarre,* and *insecure* it may be, but it's *mine!* Every bit of it! It's taken me *years* of scouting Third Avenue and the Salvation Army and auctions— (*Stepping into mess of china.*) Ouchhhhhhhhhh! (*Limps to the sofa and sits, holding her foot.*)

CASS (*Crossing to her*). Cut your foot?

ELLEN. I'm *all right.*

CASS. Got any alcohol? Or I could kiss it.

ELLEN. Don't *bother.*

CASS (*Takes champagne bottle and pours some on* ELLEN's *foot then tries to make her stretch out*). Now you just sit there nice and quiet . . . Let yourself unwind . . . Just relax . . .

(ELLEN *sinks back into corner. As he is settling her* CASS *finds the diamond necklace under a pillow, studies it.*)

You must have made the Dean's List.

(ELLEN *takes it from him and tosses it over her shoulder without comment, staring at him as if seeing him for the first time.*)

ELLEN (*Sits up, intense scrutiny, then very quiet and very steady*). Are you married?

CASS. No.

ELLEN. Let's get married. (*There is a silence.*) Do you like me?

36

CASS. Yeah—

ELLEN. You like this place?

CASS. Yeah—

ELLEN. Then let's get married.

CASS (*A pause*). You've been through an awful lot—

ELLEN. What do you say? Yes? Okay?

CASS. Well . . . I wasn't really thinking about getting married, but uh—if I thought about it at all, Betty, my secretary—

ELLEN. Are you engaged to her?

CASS. No, but—

ELLEN. Okay, then you're free. So let's get—

CASS. I thought *you* were sort of involved.

ELLEN (*Thinks about this*). I was, but no more. Listen, I'm very good around the house, cook, clean, drive a car—I'm healthy— (*Pulls her mouth open with her fingers.*)—no cavities—

CASS (*Looking into her mouth*). How about that!

ELLEN. I can sew—I can make my own clothes—when I was a school teacher I even made my own *coats*—

CASS. When you were a WHAT?

ELLEN. I was the best goddamn first grade teacher Waterbury, Connecticut ever had—my children loved me—their parents loved me—the principal loved me—I'm very good with children—if you have any I'd love them—

37

CASS. Me? Kids?

ELLEN. That's all right. Then we'll have a lot. If we need money I can always go back to teaching—I don't mind working—

CASS. You wouldn't have to— (*Catches himself.*)

ELLEN (*Crosses to desk, takes book to* CASS). And I could do some more "Esmerelda" books—I still get royalties from these—$6,000 last year—they're very popular.

CASS (*Reading cover*). "Esmerelda and the Droopy Whooping Crane." Written and illustrated by Ellen Gordon. Ellen, you're full of surprises—

ELLEN. Oh, you'd *never* be bored!

CASS. Well, why don't we think about it—

ELLEN. No, no, I don't have time. I'm *thirty years old*— (*Claps her hand over her mouth.*) I wouldn't have admitted that to my own mother—

CASS. You don't look it—

ELLEN. It just happened today . . . well, you would have found out on the license anyway. . . .

CASS. Ellen, since I met you this morning—well, I couldn't help noticing you're a very impulsive girl—

ELLEN. I *am*? Oh, this mess— (*Pointing to china on floor.*) —that doesn't mean a thing. I am the *easiest* person to get along with, honestly, I have the most *even* disposition— my friends always say, Ellen, you have the most *even* disposition—I'm really *adorable*—I mean, I'm *fun* to live with—

CASS. I think you're a helluva lot of fun—

ELLEN (*During speech takes two cigarettes and lights them*). Too much, you mean? Too much fun? Listen, I've only had *two* fiancés in my whole *life*—Jules and . . . this one. Now that's pretty goddamn clean for thirty—I'm a nice person. Sweet.

CASS. I think you're very sweet. And very nice.

ELLEN. Oh, good! Then let's not fuss, let's just go right down to City Hall— (*Puts cigarette in his mouth.*)—we could go this afternoon—

CASS (*Backing away*). This afternoon isn't good for me.

ELLEN (*Follows him*). We could be back long before eight o'clock! Then we'd be Mr. and Mrs. Henderson for real. . . . Oh, wouldn't they be surprised—

CASS (*Coughing*). She wouldn't.

ELLEN (*Laughing giddily*). *He* would! Oh, wouldn't he just! He'd be buying us our wedding supper— (*Catches herself.*) He's not the one. I don't know Mr. Cleves.

CASS (*Taking cigarette out of mouth and handing it to* ELLEN). I don't smoke.

ELLEN (*A cigarette in each hand*). I've never even met Mr. Cleves. . . . I've been in love with Mr. Cleves ever since I came back from around the world. Mr. Cleves is—*was* my fiancé. Before you. After Jules . . . (*Disappointed.*) You're not surprised.

39

CASS. I kind of figured he was the one. After Jules.

ELLEN. Mr. Cleves always thought I'd make a good wife. He'd have married me himself long ago if it weren't for his children . . . it's his tough luck. . . . But he'll be nice. *Time* magazine says he has the ruthlessness of an eagle, but he's sweet with balloons. . . .

CASS. Exactly how do you mean that?

ELLEN. You see, I wouldn't have anything to do with him for about a year after we met because he was married. Then I got hepatitis, and he came to the hospital every day, *every* day—read to me—we talked—I told him I'd always wanted a whole room full of balloons because it would be so gay, you know? Well, the day I was discharged, he brought me home—here—nothing but balloons, wall to wall and floor to ceiling. . . . That did it. Two years of Wednesdays.

CASS. You're still in love with him—

ELLEN. No, no. That's all over and I'm going to devote myself to you and spend my life making you happy. (*Puts cigarette in his mouth.*) You mustn't be jealous of memories. I can think of Mr. Cleves and balloons, and my lawnmower, with nothing but fondness. (*Crosses to corner and pulls out lawnmower as* CASS *stubs out cigarette.*) This is my favorite present. I have my very own garden.

CASS (*Looks out*). Gee, I never heard of wisteria blooming in July, either. What do you feed it? Raw meat?

ELLEN. The blossoms aren't real. They're some kind of plastic. I bought them at Bloomingdale's and tied them on. You can't tell, can you? From here, anyway. For the winter I change to poinsettias.

CASS. You *are* kind of adorable.

ELLEN. Oh, you'll *like* me! And I'll be so happy not being alone any more that I'll be a doll. I'm so excited—I'm so warm —I can't stand it—

CASS. If you had a screw driver I could fix your air conditioner for you—

ELLEN. You could? (*Crosses to chest.*) Well I do. (*Rummaging.*) Right here some place—

CASS. You got yourself a real handy man. I used to be a construction worker summers to put myself through college, and construction workers can do anything. Everybody knows that.

ELLEN (*Finds screw driver, gives it to* CASS). Here it is. You went to college?

CASS (*Busily working on air conditioner*). Yeah. I'm educated. Half. Junior college. Got an athletic scholarship. Football, baseball, basketball, and track. . . . All this needed was a small adjustment. There you are.

ELLEN (*Delighted*). You mean it's fixed? And I was going to have to wait until Monday for a man to come—

CASS. Press the button.

(ELLEN *presses button, there is a hum of operating machinery and then a loud explosion and a puff of smoke.*)

CASS (*Rushes to turn machine off, opens garden door to drive*

out the smoke, takes a fortifying drink of champagne). You
said Monday?

ELLEN *(Managing to be admiring).* Well, I think it's nice that
you're so handy anyway. Oh, lots of people are going to
be surprised by us! Wait'll you meet my mother—

CASS *(Looks around nervously).* Where is she?

ELLEN. Back home in Waterbury with her color T.V. Cass, let's
fill the house with children, lots of them, right away.

CASS. You know, you act like a humminghird, but you've got
the soul of a little brown hen. Just can't wait to climb into
the nest and sit down, can you?

ELLEN *(Ignoring this).* Would you like to see what I looked
like as a baby to get some idea of what to expect? *(Starts
for closet.)* I've got a family album—Mother's in it, too.
*(Opens closet door and an enormous bunch of balloons
spills out.* ELLEN *gasps.)*

*(Holding balloons by end of string so that they float high
over her head.)* He loves me . . . Oh dear God the sweet
man—he must have got up in the middle of the night with
his little helium kit . . . blowing up all these balloons . . .
Coming to the hospital every day when I was so *yellow*—
My necklace!— *(Finds necklace, puts it in breast pocket.)*
—Bringing picnic lunches in his little briefcase. *(Notices*
CASS.*)* What are you still doing here?

CASS. I'm waiting for my call. . . . Look, Ellen, I'm going to
level with you. There isn't any friend . . . I *had* to do it,
Ellen—

ELLEN *(Embracing balloons protectively).* You tricked me!

CASS. Will you listen to me?

ELLEN. . . . If it hadn't been for these balloons, you'd be the father of my children . . .

CASS. Listen to me! I own a plant, Henderson Machine and Tool, right? Six months ago Cleves bought us—

ELLEN. Well? What's that got to do with anything?

CASS. He double-crossed us, that's what! Look, we make E-Z Pull Drawer Slides—

ELLEN. Easy what?

CASS (*Crosses to chest, yanks at balky drawer*). E-Z Pull Drawer Slides—"The answer to the housewife's problem." He bought us to put us out of business, to get himself a tax loss— He's ignored our letters, won't take our calls— I had to come to New York because I've *got* to see him, it's our only chance.

ELLEN. You got paid, didn't you?

CASS. Come *on*, Ellen. George and I built that plant with our bare hands— How would *you* feel if you were going to lose *this* place? Would *you* rather have money? The only way I can save our plant is to see Cleves, and the way I figure it now, I can see Cleves by being right here in this place at eight o'clock tonight . . .

ELLEN. . . . I don't understand business at all, but I will go to a movie so you can use my place.

CASS. Thanks.

ELLEN. Not at all.

CASS (*A pause, turns away, plows through china*). Do you

happen to have a dust pan and a broom in this loony bin?

ELLEN. I suggest you look in the kitchen. (CASS *exists to kitchen.* ELLEN, *still clutching balloons runs to phone, dials.*) Darling? I know I'm not supposed to call you, but I had to tell you— The balloons were just the sweetest. . . . It's been a trying day for both of us, love, but I had to tell you how much I love you. . . . Darling, talk slower, you sound so frantic. . . . What? Out of here by Monday? Dearest . . . (ELLEN *lets go of balloons and they rise to the ceiling.*) . . . have you lost your mind? John, may I say something? This is my *home*, I *live* here, remember? You *know* how I love everything in it, you *know* what it means to me. Are you actually telling me I have to *give* this up—MOVE OUT—because YOUR wife wants to RE-DECORATE? (*Slams down phone, throws ash tray, runs off into bedroom.*)

CASS (*Entering from the kitchen with a dust pan and broom*).

Ellen? Are you breaking up the joint again? Ellen?

ELLEN (*Opens bedroom door*). *You* and *I* are going to *dinner* at *Pavillon* tonight! (*Exits, slamming door, immediately opens it, darts out.*) DEAR! (*Exits, slamming door.*)

FAST CURTAIN

44

ACT ONE

Scene 2

PLACE: *The same.*

TIME: *7:30 that evening.*

AT RISE: *The mess of china and the balloons have been cleared. There are several beer cans on the coffee table.* CASS *is on the terrace, mowing the lawn.*

After a moment ELLEN *rushes on from the bedroom in a terry cloth robe and shower cap, goes to the coffee table and clears all but one beer can, turns and runs to exit to the kitchen on her line.*

ELLEN. Cass? You can have the bathroom now. I'm all ready.

CASS (*Entering from the terrace with the mower and returning it to its corner*). After dinner when it's cooled off some we'd better run the sprinkler . . . leave it on all night.

45

(*Crosses to coffee table, takes beer can, and drinks.* ELLEN *re-enters from kitchen and puts tablecloth on dining table.*)

I thought you said you were all ready!

ELLEN. I am. Underneath. Cass, do I look nervous?

CASS. No, you don't look nervous . . . but your hands do.

ELLEN. I'll wear gloves. I wish my hat had a veil. All over my face. Cass, please hurry! I want you to check me out before they get here. It's very important—

CASS (*Exiting to bedroom*). Okay, okay, stop worrying, you'll be fine . . .

ELLEN (*To herself*). I'll be fine . . .

(ELLEN *crosses to coffee table, blows dust off, crosses to desk, puts "Esmerelda" books on window seat, crosses to dining table, takes off cloth, exits kitchen. There is a moment, and* JOHN *enters with key. He has changed to a dark suit.*)

JOHN (*Calling*). Ellen—

(ELLEN *re-enters with cloth.*)

(*Relieved.*) You're *not* going! Well! I'm delighted to see you've come to your senses. I was stunned when Dorothy told me—I wouldn't believe you'd actually come to dinner with—

ELLEN (*Quietly icy*). John, I *won't* move out on Monday!

JOHN. Pet, I've decided exactly what to do. You'll go to a hotel, the St. Regis, have a little holiday, and when she's finished, you'll move back.

46

ELLEN (*Folding cloth and putting it in chest*). I don't like hotels. I want to stay here, and I want everything exactly as it is. (*Starting to bedroom*). She's going to *murder* my grass.

JOHN. A couple of men working one day can easily take up the flagstone and put down sod— Actually it's much better.

ELLEN. I don't want sod. (*Exits bedroom.*)

(*Off.*) I made that grass— (*Re-enters without shower cap, with shoes, steps into them.*) Every blade means something to me—just as much as my chair and my table and my—oh, John! My *furniture!* (*Exits bedroom.*)

JOHN (*Calling*). Sweetheart, I'll have a truck pick up everything and store it in one of our warehouses. As soon as Dorothy's finished we'll move all the new things out and all the old things back. . . . (JOHN *sags at the realization of the task and sinks into a chair. To himself.*) Oh, my God!

ELLEN (*Re-enters in dinner dress, clutching the diamond necklace as she struggles to reach the back zipper*). That should be very simple. The Cleves Cannery trucks will steal back and forth in the dead of night, I suppose, so no one will ever know—but a bright yellow ten-ton truck *is* conspicuous.

JOHN (*Noticing her dress*). Going somewhere?

ELLEN. Of course. (*Crosses to mirror, adjusts necklace.*) To dinner at Pavillon—

JOHN. Ellen, stop playing games.

ELLEN. I'm not! After all, John, I've got to do *something* to cheer myself up—losing my home on my birthday—

47

JOHN. You are *not* losing your home! Can't you understand simple *expediency?*

(CASS, *clothed only in a large, flowered bath towel, starts out of bedroom, sees* JOHN, *turns back to bedroom, changes mind, and enters room.*)

CASS. Uh . . . excuse me. Uh . . . my . . . (*Crosses to suitcase.*) . . . clean shirt . . . excuse me . . . how do you do. (*Extends hand.*)

ELLEN (*Very social as* JOHN *ignores* CASS's *hand*). Oh, I don't believe you've met, have you? John, this is Cass Henderson. Cass, John Cleves. (*To* CASS.) Darling, do hurry. You're an old slowpoke.

CASS (*Zipping up her dress*). I am hurrying.

JOHN. What the *Hell* do you think you're doing?

CASS. She can't reach—

ELLEN. He's just zipping up his wife's dress, John.

JOHN. Zipping up his wife's dress— What is he doing here? Has he been here all afternoon?

CASS. I've been waiting to talk to you, Mr. Cleves. I wrote you six letters—

JOHN. I never received any letters—

CASS. Oh yes you did! The last three were sent special delivery-registered-certified. I've got the signed receipts right— (*Gropes for non-existent pockets.*) Right— (*Pats suitcase.*)

ELLEN (*Pushing him toward bedroom*). Cass, please! Not now!

CASS (*Crossing to bedroom with suitcase*). Well, I've got them.

JOHN (*Pointing to entrance door*). That way—

ELLEN. John, he's got to get dressed.

CASS. I'm not finished with you, Cleves. (*Exits bedroom.*)

JOHN. *He's* not finished with *me?* Was he here all afternoon? Just the two of you? Alone? What the hell does he think he's doing?

ELLEN (*Elegant, ladylike*). He's being my husband to protect you from *your* wife, that's what he's doing. It's all for you — Where *is* Dorothy?

JOHN (*Glances at watch*). She'll be here any minute. (*Pleading, affectionate.*) Angel, I know you're annoyed—perhaps you even have some reason—you're hurt, angry—but think what you're doing to *us!* For a momentary hurt, easily remedied—*believe* me, I swear to you everything here will be the same again—

ELLEN. It's no good, John. It won't work.

JOHN. Of course it'll work.

ELLEN. Us. We won't work.

JOHN. Pet, this is hardly the time to rehash—

CASS (*At bedroom door, clad in trousers, bare-chested and barefoot, unwrapping a clean shirt. He has three postal receipts in his hand, which he puts in his mouth when he*

49

needs both hands for the shirt). You want to see those receipts?

JOHN. Henderson, you are one of the most vicious young men I have ever—

CASS. Vicious! Look who's calling who VICIOUS!

ELLEN (*As she passes* JOHN, *icy*). Excuse me. (*Momentarily defeated, takes shirt wrappings from* CASS, *exits bedroom.*)

JOHN. —One of the most vicious young men I have ever encountered. But since you are here, I will tell you that I took a look at our files on your company this afternoon—

CASS. Oh, you did! And you still think I'm vicious? When you know all about me—

JOHN. I don't "know all about you" and I certainly shouldn't care to. I do know that you make some sort of a gadget— (CASS *puts shirt on.*)

CASS. E-Z Pull Drawer Slides.

JOHN. E-Z Pull what?

(ELLEN *enters from bedroom with large hat. Crosses to mirror with it.*)

CASS. E-Z Pull Drawer Slides.

JOHN. —Some gadget—and that there's a perfectly reasonable reason—

ELLEN (*Deliberately interrupting to get* JOHN's *attention as way to exit bedroom*). Excuse me.

JOHN. —Why we're closing you down next week—

CASS. SURE! To get rid of competition and establish a TAX loss—

JOHN. Henderson, when I buy a company, and I buy them by the dozens—every piece of information about that company —rate of growth, efficiency of personnel, unit cost of items produced—that sort of thing—it's all fed into a 607—

ELLEN (*Gives up, turns and brushes by* JOHN *and* CASS *on way to exit bedroom*). Excuse me.

CASS. A six-oh—what?

JOHN. A 607 computer. Couple of minutes, out comes the answer. Apparently, the Cleves complex can function better without Henderson Machine and Tool. There's nothing personal about it. The machine indicates a procedural pattern and—

CASS. Hiding behind a machine! Nothing personal! Your people came to Akron six months ago, sweet-talked us into selling—gave us three-year contracts to stay on and manage the plant—*three-year contracts*—

(ELLEN *has entered from bedroom carrying* CASS'S *shoes and socks. Crosses to* JOHN, *waves them defiantly in his face.*)

JOHN. You'll be paid off in full.

(ELLEN *gives* CASS *his shoes. Turns and exits to bedroom.*)

CASS. I'm not a football coach! I haven't had a losing season! I don't want to get paid off! I've got a winning plant!

JOHN (*Gazes after* ELLEN). The 607 indicates—

CASS (*Teetering on one foot to put on socks and shoes*). The hell with your 607! My brother George has four daughters who want a college education—a mother-in-law who's always in the hospital—so your people come along, and George sees a chance for some ready cash and we can still run the business. All right, I made a mistake!!! I let him talk me into it! But you gave us three-year contracts, and I thought—

JOHN. Business is business! For Christ's sake, you made a deal! Now take your money and— (*Exploding.*) —go build another business! (ELLEN *enters from bedroom with long gloves, which she proceeds to put on under* JOHN's *nose.*)

CASS. Build another business? That's what you'd do! Screw your business! Screw everybody! SCREW THE WORLD! Listen, I want George's kids to get to college—

JOHN. Henderson, control yourself! This is neither the time nor the place—

CASS. This is the only time and the only place—

ELLEN. John, this is the only time for us . . . I mean, what we were talking about is much more important than—

JOHN. No, Ellen, no. First things first, and the first thing on my agenda— (*Crosses to* CASS.) —is *you*, Henderson. For the last time, will you *get out?*

(*Crosses to door, opens it to reveal* DOROTHY, *hand raised, ready to knock, dressed as in previous scene, carrying large paper bag.*)

DOROTHY. John! You're early! (*To* CASS.) Hello there, have you met—

ELLEN. Yes, we introduced ourselves. How nice to see you, Mrs. Cleves.

DOROTHY. Aren't you beautiful! And Mr. Henderson. . . .

CASS. Excuse me. Be right out. (*Exits to bedroom.*)

DOROTHY. Well, it's been a long day, but a satisfying one. (*Drawing a swatch out of bag.*) Dear, I'm sure you'll approve of these.

JOHN. Dorothy, can't that wait?

DOROTHY. If that isn't just like a man! When I've spent the entire day—well, *I* like them and I'm sure Mrs. Henderson, as another woman, will, too. (*Pulls out other swatches.*) Subtle, muted, unobtrusive—they'll give the room a certain *je ne sais quoi*—God knows it needs it.

ELLEN (*Flat*). They're lovely.

DOROTHY (*Draping swatches on sofa*). Dear, do you suppose the Modern would let us borrow back some of our things we let them borrow? The van Gogh would really pull it all together and it would be nice for the clients.

JOHN (*Sinks into chair*). They're on permanent loan for tax purposes—I don't know—I have no idea. Call the Museum.

ELLEN (*Calling*). Darling! (CASS *steps out of bedroom as* JOHN *turns to* ELLEN *and quickly turns away before* DOROTHY *notices.*) Darling, why don't you offer our guests a drink? (*Takes off hat.*)

DOROTHY (*Still busy with swatches, now at window seat*). What a splendid idea!

ELLEN. There's champagne—

53

CASS (*Helpful*). Beer.

ELLEN. —Scotch, gin, bourbon—

DOROTHY. Champagne! I always feel when you start with champagne you should really go on with it—and it's so party—

ELLEN. Mr. Cleves?

JOHN. Scotch. Double. Neat.

DOROTHY. Oh, John! If you had champagne with us— It's Mrs. Henderson's birthday party and we could all toast her—it's so much friendlier. (*To* CASS.) Champagne for everyone.

CASS (*Crossing to kitchen*). That's easy to remember. (*As* ELLEN *joins him.*) I can manage, sweetheart. (*Hugs her.*)

ELLEN. I know you can, darling, but I'm going to whip up that dip you're so crazy about. (*Winks at* JOHN, *exits with* CASS.)

DOROTHY (*Very busy draping on every available space*). I wonder if she's going to do it with her gloves on.

JOHN. When I want a double scotch neat, I want a double scotch neat! Not champagne! I happen to *need* a double scotch nea—

DOROTHY (*Crosses to get pills from purse*). You're getting tired-cranky, dear—though you look fresh as can be—changed at the office, didn't you? Oh, you're just suffering from your regular Thursday night fatigue. But you'll see champagne'll put you in a party mood.

JOHN. *Nothing* would put me in a party mood.

DOROTHY (*Crosses to* JOHN). I have something here that will. From Miss Linsley. She said she'd offered you a Benzedrine and you'd refused. But these are much better. (*Gives* JOHN *pills.*) They're such a dear little couple—you'll enjoy them. (*Crosses to kitchen, opens door, and calls.*) May I have a small glass of water? Aren't you busy!

What a garish color! I suppose it's meant to be cheerful.

(*Taking water from* CASS.) Thank you so much.

(*Crossing to* JOHN.) She *is* doing it with her gloves on.

JOHN. You know I never take pills. What are these things? It looks like a kaleidoscope.

DOROTHY. Miss Linsley said the colors keep popping off and each pop is a *charge* of energy.

JOHN. Miss Linsley! Have you had them analyzed? (*Puts vial in pocket.*)

DOROTHY (*Puts glass on chest*). All right, John, I was just trying to help you. Isn't she a dramatic little thing! Big hats, long gloves, diamonds—that necklace is rather bad taste, actually. (*Takes* ELLEN's *hat from table, crosses to mirror with it, tries it on.*) Her family must have money and he's trying to live up to them. (*Returning hat to table.*) About my coat—

JOHN. If you haven't learned by now that my tax bracket does not allow for foolish luxuries—(*Catches himself, remembering his speech to* ELLEN *that morning.*)

DOROTHY. All right, John, we'll talk about it later. You know, I'm going to keep the sofa, it's not bad really, and those two little chairs, perhaps. . . . If you'd just take a pill, you'd be feeling tip-top in a moment.

JOHN. I'll never feel tip-top again—I refuse to.

DOROTHY (*Moving furniture*). I don't understand you—really
I don't. You trained me ever since I was a bride to be nice
to the client, and for the *first* time in all these *dreary* client
years it's no effort—

JOHN. I don't have to be nice. I own him.

DOROTHY. You must have *meant* to be nice. They're here. And
there's no need to be rude. I know you're tired and you've
had a horrendous day—

JOHN. What do you mean, horrendous? It's been a perfectly
ordinary workday—all days are alike when you're an eagle—
(*Catches himself.*)

DOROTHY (*Moving sofa*). Eagles must have good days and bad
days, too.

JOHN. Dorothy, will you stop fidgeting! Fidgeting and babbling
and babbling and fidgeting—

DOROTHY (*Takes a beat, considers him, her face softens, she
crosses to him, then very sympathetic and tender*). It's the
horse, isn't it? Miss Linsley told me. Dreadful men—how
dare they? Outbidding you on Sweet Sam and then calling
you to taunt you about it—long distance—collect.

JOHN (*Opportunistically seizing the moment, plays it to the
hilt*). You're very perceptive. . . . It's the horse.

DOROTHY. Why don't you just offer those nasty syndicate people
more money and buy him back? Wouldn't that be easy?

JOHN. Too easy . . . Where's the fun? (*Absently patting her
fanny.*) You know how I am . . .

56

(DOROTHY *moves away as* CASS *enters with tray of glasses and bottle of champagne, but not before he has seen* JOHN's *affectionate gesture.* ELLEN *enters behind* CASS, *carrying a small bowl and basket of potato chips.*)

ELLEN. I hope you'll like this—

CASS. Sure they will. Ellen's known all over Akron for her dip— (*Pours.*)

ELLEN (*Trying valiantly to scoop up dip*). This is what I gave Cass's softball team—the Akron Athletic Club—when they won the championship—they just loved it! They said, Mrs. Henderson, this sure is good— (*Defeated.*) I think I made it a little thin.

(CASS *serves* ELLEN *and then* JOHN.)

It's more of a winter thing, really—we always serve it with hot buttered rum after we've been skating on the lake.

DOROTHY. You have a lake?

ELLEN. We don't—Lake Erie.

DOROTHY. Lake Erie? I didn't know Akron was on Lake Erie.

CASS (*Quickly*). That's what we call the lake where we go skating—eerie.

DOROTHY. Oh dear, here I am forgetting— (*Takes small package from purse, gives it to* ELLEN.) Happy birthday from John and me. And if you'd prefer something else, Cartier is terribly nice about exchanges.

ELLEN (*Very still*). . . . I'm sure I'll like . . . Thank you, Mrs. Cleves. . . .

DOROTHY (*Turning* JOHN *to* ELLEN). It's from John, too.

57

ELLEN. Thank you too, Mr. Cleves.

DOROTHY. I wanted you to remember today. It didn't start well, but I'm so happy to see you two so . . . well . . . just remember what I told you this morning.

ELLEN (*Has gotten box opened and takes out a small pillbox, looks at it, stricken*). I've never had a pillbox. . . .

DOROTHY. Splendid! Now, a toast! John?

JOHN (*Flat*). Many happy returns . . .

(*They sip as* ELLEN *stands frozen.*)

DOROTHY (*Crossing to dip*). I must taste this. It looks simply delicious! (*Makes a noble effort, but is unsuccessful.*)

ELLEN. Would you mind if I didn't go along to dinner? I—

DOROTHY. What is it, dear? What's wrong?

ELLEN. Oh—nothing—I just think it would be better if I stayed here—

CASS. You all right?

ELLEN. I'm fine! Well, I'm not, really—it's just that I never had a pillbox before.

JOHN. If Mrs. Henderson doesn't feel up to—

DOROTHY. But she *has* to! It's her party! I stopped there today and spoke to Soulé and he's prepared all *sorts* of surprises. He'd be so disappointed—*we'd* be so disappointed—

JOHN. Dorothy, I'm sure Mrs. Henderson can make up her own mind—

DOROTHY (*Cautioning*). John. . . . (*Crosses to* ELLEN.) I don't know what you two said to each other in the kitchen, but I'm afraid you've been naughty again. My dear, you've got to come along. The moment you're in that beautiful room— it's so stuffy in here—with all those sweet, hovering waiters who really care— (*Drawing* ELLEN *along, arm around her.*) Do you good. Shall we go? Oh, your beautiful dip! Why don't we take it with us?

ELLEN. It's too thin—not enough paprika, I guess.

DOROTHY. It looks simply delicious! Now, you'll see, we're going to have a lovely evening. Get your hat, Mrs. Henderson. (*Taking* ELLEN *to door.*) After dinner we'll go to Shepheard's—it's a madly chic little place with records and musicians—we can dance— (ELLEN *looks back helplessly as she is propelled through the door by* DOROTHY.)

CASS (*Patronizingly*). Come on, Mr. Cleves, it's a double date.

(*Exits.* JOHN *takes bottle of pills from his pocket and takes pill as* THE CURTAIN IS LOWERED.)

ACT TWO

Scene 1

PLACE: *The same.*

TIME: *Later that same evening.*

AT RISE: *The stage is empty. Moonlight and street light shine through the garden door. This is the only illumination on stage. Voices are heard in the hallway, and, after a moment* CASS *unlocks the door. The hallway is illuminated, and we see the figures in silhouette.*

ELLEN *enters and turns on the lights, then crosses to the coffee table to begin cleaning up.* DOROTHY *enters just behind* ELLEN, *followed by* JOHN. *They all look strained and tense.*

DOROTHY (*On her entrance*). John is such a party-poop. Arguing all through dinner and then refusing to take us any place gay—*refusing!* We could have danced!

CASS. That's all right, Mrs. Cleves. Ellen and I were dancing this afternoon, right here. Got all tuckered out. (*Slaps* JOHN *on the arm to annoy him.*) Gosh that dinner—

ELLEN (*Flat*). It was delicious!

DOROTHY. Henri Soulé surpassed himself this evening. The soufflé Grand Marnier with candles . . . he said it couldn't be done, but he did it!

ELLEN. It was delicious!

JOHN. Dorothy, I think we should leave.

DOROTHY (*With forced pleasantness*). Why don't you take a pill, John. (*Takes* CASS's *arm, starts for garden.*) Mr. Henderson, when you were a construction worker did you ever have any experience with flagstone? Would you know how much I'd need to cover this place?

CASS. Well . . . I'd have to guess at the measurements—

(*Flips on garden light. They exit to the garden.* CASS *closes the door.*)

ELLEN. I didn't want to go.

JOHN. Pity you didn't realize that earlier in the day—

ELLEN. I'm just not sophisticated—

JOHN. That's part of your charm.

ELLEN. It was awful. And then when she said she's got her own truck to take all my things away—to be auctioned like slaves at an auction gallery—I don't even know which one! She said she wouldn't *embarrass* Parke Bernet—

JOHN. Now don't get emotional. I'll find out which gallery it is, fill the place with my top men—they'll be thoroughly briefed. My accountant will undoubtedly resign, but you'll get everything back.

ELLEN. John, I'm leaving you.

JOHN. Pet, you've felt this way before and you've always—

ELLEN. No. This time I mean it. Now that I've met . . . her . . . it's quite different. I'm ashamed of myself. She's a nice woman. When she gave me that pillbox from both of you I—I wanted to kill myself—

JOHN. You're dramatizing.

ELLEN. Two people thought of me today: you and your wife. Mother forgot. (*Crosses to window seat.*) Well, I'm not wasting any more of my life. Next year'll be different. I'm going to find a husband somewhere and have a lot of children, and they'll gather round me and bake a cake—

(*Sits on the window seat.* DOROTHY *and* CASS *come into view on the terrace.* JOHN *sees them, crosses to window seat, takes an "Esmerelda" book and opens it.*)

You've been saying for years that one of us should be strong enough to break it off. Tonight I'm strong.

JOHN. Darling, this is too big to talk about now—with them— (*His gesture toward* DOROTHY *and* CASS *elicits a responding wave from* DOROTHY.)

ELLEN. This is the time, John, with them—with *her*—she gives me the strength—

JOHN (*Taking it in stride*). Obviously you're hysterical, and that's why you mustn't make a decision now. Give yourself time to think it over.

ELLEN. I've had two years. Junior college is enough for me. No, John. Can't you understand? I'm through. We are. Finished. Forever. (*Exiting to kitchen with tray.*) Excuse me. (ELLEN *re-enters.*) You really lost him?

JOHN. Lost who?

ELLEN. Sweet Sam. You mentioned it at dinner. I am sorry.

JOHN. You think my mind is on a— (DOROTHY *enters.*) —horse?

DOROTHY (*Crosses rapidly to get her notebook from her purse. ELLEN sits in dining chair*). I must get my notebook. Mr. Henderson is telling me just how I can put a fountain out there—What a clever husband you have, my dear . . . (*Exits.*)

JOHN (*Crosses to dining table*). Ellen, do you mind if I face the garden? (ELLEN *rises, takes other chair.*) What will you do? Where will you go?

ELLEN. Go? . . . I'm just leaving *you*, John.

JOHN (*Stunned silence*). . . . You mean you'd stay here?

ELLEN. Of course. It's my home. It was my home before I even met you.

JOHN. Yes, I know, I appreciate that. But you realize that on Monday Dorothy—

ELLEN. Not now. Not when I'm giving her *you*.

JOHN. But, pet, she doesn't know that.

ELLEN. Tell her.

JOHN. Sweetheart, you need a change. A week or ten days at the St. Regis'll do you a world of good.

ELLEN. John, I am not moving out. You'll have to do something about Dorothy. That's your problem. I've got my own. And by the way, I'd like my apartment back. In my name. That's all I want. (*Unfastens necklace.*) Nothing else. (*Tosses necklace to him.*)

JOHN (*Giving it back*). Pet . . . it's yours.

(*She tosses it back.*)

I don't want it. (JOHN *gives it to her.*)

ELLEN. You'll have to take it back. (*She gives it back.*) It would give you—

(*He gives it back to her.*)

—an excuse to call. (*She throws it on table.*) All right, leave it there. Now there are a few details—the apartment—

JOHN. Pet, it's yours just as much as it ever was.

ELLEN. It's not mine when it's owned by Cleves. I want it in *my* name. Don't say it's impossible. I'll buy it from Cleves. All right, then, I'll sell my Cleves stock and if that isn't enough—I'll—I'll— (*Inspired.*) —you could sell me my apartment and take a loss!

JOHN. Oh my God!

ELLEN (*Bewildered*). But I thought the best thing to *have* is a loss!

65

JOHN. Yes, but it's got to *look* legitimate! First, you sell a block of Cleves stock—how did you acquire said stock? You bought it. And from what source did you acquire the money to purchase this stock? Source unknown. Then immediately following your sale of our shares, we sell you a company property at a loss. Why the Treasury boys would start an investigation—blow the whole thing wide open! You see, angel, you *can't* leave me.

ELLEN. Oh, yes I can. There must be some way. Your accountant would know—any tax genius—

(DOROTHY *enters from garden.* JOHN *tries to hide necklace.* CASS *stands at door.*)

DOROTHY (*Crossing to* JOHN). I'm so excited! The fountain's going to be heaven! Mr. Henderson drew the plans for me. And one more thing, John, could we commission what's-his-name—that sculptor who makes the big gold wire things—Lippold!—something for the center of the back wall, something with a mirror behind it—

JOHN (*Preoccupied with necklace*). Oh yes, Lippold—

DOROTHY (*Jubilant*). You're a darling! Aren't you two having a nice chat! Well, we'll join you in a minute—we're just about finished here— (*Exits. Closes door.*)

JOHN. You know it has nothing to do with Dorothy. I like Dorothy.

ELLEN. So do I.

JOHN. But I love you and I want you—I want you all the time, not just Wednesdays. You can't imagine what it's been like for me—leaving you, going home, wanting to come here instead. . . . But when I go into their rooms at night to be sure that they're covered and I see those little arms flung over those little heads. . . .

ELLEN. Each time you talk about them they get smaller and smaller.

JOHN. Pet, I won't let you do this to us! Let me come back to-night.

ELLEN. You can't. It isn't Wednesday. And I wouldn't let you if you could.

JOHN (*Clasping necklace on* ELLEN's *neck*). I'll tell Dorothy I have to stay in town to work. I'll send her back to Short Hills. We can't end it this way. You've got to give me a chance to talk it over.

(DOROTHY *and* CASS *enter*.)

DOROTHY (*To* CASS). You've been so patient. John, that garden is going to be something *Town and Country* will *beg* to photograph. Heavens, I've gotten quite grimy. May I—

ELLEN. Would you like to freshen up? (*Rises and starts for bedroom.*) We dressed in a hurry . . . it's a little messy —(*Throws this at* JOHN.)

DOROTHY (*Following*). Don't worry about that! (*As they exit.*) You know, I haven't seen the bedroom yet—

JOHN (*As soon as they exit*). I've had just about enough of you, you clever construction worker. Get OUT!

CASS. I'm not leaving! Not until you tell me we keep the plant open and George and me stay on to manage—

JOHN. NO! But I will tell you that I find you a fantastic bore at a dinner table. The unabridged story of your dreary life as you consumed an entire chicken for two is completely forgettable.

CASS. Mrs. Cleves wasn't bored.

JOHN. Mrs. Cleves happens to be obsessed with the idea that we should be closer to the "simple little people." An obsession I don't share. Now, GET OUT!

CASS. You're forgetting one thing that's kind of important. I'm calling the shots now. I can wipe you out with just a few well-chosen words to Mrs. Cleves. Put *that* in your old 607!

JOHN (*A pause, then calm and sure*). But you're not going to do that.

CASS. I'm not? What the hell have I got to lose?

JOHN. You won't because you can't. That's *my* kind of ploy, not yours.

DOROTHY (*Enters from bedroom and crosses to them*). Will you two STOP talking *business!* John, you did your best to ruin dinner with your wrangling and refused to do anything gay afterward—John, have you *seen* that *bedroom?*—It's her birthday, and this is her party and the very least we can do is be jolly and how can we be jolly if we're not friendly? (*To* CASS.) I'm convinced he wouldn't be quite so overbearing if he had some contact with the world at large—the simple, *little* people.

JOHN (*Taunting*). Well, Henderson?

CASS. Mrs. Cleves . . . (*Gives up, starts for kitchen, unable to look at* JOHN.) —uh—you were about to order a brandy at the restaurant when we had to leave. There's some here. Would you like—?

DOROTHY. Splendid idea!

(CASS *exits.*)

JOHN (*Looking after* CASS). Gutless bastard—now he's being ingratiating, too.

DOROTHY (*Folding swatches*). How can you be jolly with that mental attitude?

JOHN. I'm not jolly, and I *will* not be jolly.

DOROTHY. You'll make an effort, John. Take a pill.

(ELLEN *enters from bedroom dressed in a hostess gown.*)

Heavens, either you brought a trunk or you're a shark at packing! It's divine!

ELLEN. I feel more like a hostess in this.

DOROTHY (*Woman to woman, ignoring* JOHN). My dear, I hope you won't think me presumptuous, but although we just met this morning, I feel very close to you somehow. . . . I know something's troubling you.

ELLEN (*Brightly*). Oh no! Nothing. I'm fine. Everything's fine.

DOROTHY (*Folding swatch, passes over this*). Perhaps if you told me about it I could help you.

ELLEN (*Glances at* JOHN). I'd like to tell you . . . but I can't . . .

DOROTHY. I'm sorry. There *are* some things too private to tell to anyone.

ELLEN. Oh, it's not that. I'd be glad to— (*Blurts out.*) I'm leaving the man I love.

(JOHN *is startled.*)

DOROTHY. How long have you been married?

(ELLEN *holds up two fingers.*)

Two years, isn't it? My dear, that's a *moment* in a lifetime! You still have so much to learn about each other.

ELLEN. No, no, you don't understand—

(JOHN *tries to catch* ELLEN's *eye.*)

DOROTHY (*Unwilling to be interrupted*). Dear, let me finish. Living with any man is difficult, living with anyone at all! And marriage is not living happily ever after as the books would lead us to think. (*Sympathetic glance at* JOHN.) Marriage is compromise. Now, I adore bright colors, John loathes them. He can't bear them, I don't wear them. Compromise.

ELLEN. That's compromise?

JOHN (*Swiftly*). Of course.

DOROTHY. Another thing, John *loves* to play games—his favorite pastime of an evening. It wasn't mine when I married him—but I've learned to enjoy them, too.

(CASS *enters with tray, bottle of brandy, and glasses.*)

(*Swiftly.*) Give it a chance—give *him* a chance.

JOHN. Dorothy, I think we should leave.

DOROTHY. Why don't we play a game? What shall we play?

JOHN. Any other time I'd be delighted—

(CASS *gives brandy to* JOHN, DOROTHY, *and* ELLEN.)

DOROTHY (*Warning*). John! (*To* ELLEN.) It's *your* birthday and *your* party. You choose. What about charades?

JOHN. Dorothy, NO!

DOROTHY. Oh, of course, dear, I forgot. (*Confidentially to* EL-LEN.) John has one of those disc things that pop in and out at the most inopportune times. I've always suspected it's psychosomatic, but at that age they all have something. All right, we'll be sedentary. The match game they played in the Marienbad film! All we need is lots of matches.

CASS. There should be some in here.

(*Rises and leads way to kitchen;* DOROTHY *eagerly follows.*)

DOROTHY. I want a word with you, young man— It's based on mathematical formulas, you know, and I find it utterly fascinating! I majored in math at Bryn Mawr.

(*They are off. During the following scene we hear their voices off.*)

JOHN. Now what are you doing?

ELLEN (*Cold*). Being a sophisticated hostess, like the jet set, you know? . . . I don't know what I'm doing. She's like the way I wish my mother was—I don't know—I just wanted to tell her the truth.

JOHN. Good God!

ELLEN. John, I don't like you. I resent what you're doing to her—to both of us.

71

JOHN. You may not *like* me at the moment, but you're so confused you're forgetting that we *love* each other!

ELLEN. That's the heartbreak! But you're hurting her, and I'm part of it.

JOHN. But she doesn't *know* I'm hurting her, so I'm not. (*Takes* ELLEN *by the shoulders.*) Is that a happy woman? Is she? You see? We're not hurting her, we're not taking anything away from her. In point of fact, having you in my life makes me happy, a happy husband for Dorothy! Far from hurting her, pet, we're *helping* her.

ELLEN. We are?

JOHN. Of course! If I didn't have you, Dorothy would be *miserable!*

ELLEN (*Considers this*). Well, I don't want to hurt her, but why should I help her? I mean, she's a nice woman and everything, but she's still your wife—

JOHN. You see how confused you are? Pet, we've got to talk. (*Hastily as* DOROTHY *is about to enter.*) I'm coming back later. Get rid of him.

DOROTHY (*Off*). Beginnings are always hard.

(*Enters with box of large kitchen matches. Over her shoulder to* CASS.) Children make a big difference.

(*To* JOHN *and* ELLEN.) We're back with the spoils! Enough matches so that we can all play until dawn! (*She seats herself on the sofa.*)

JOHN. I don't want to play.

DOROTHY. John, it's one of your favorites!

72

JOHN. I'm bored with it. I don't want to play.

DOROTHY. All right, dear, all right. Then how about ghost? You haven't played that in a while.

JOHN. I don't think we should. It's getting late.

DOROTHY. It's not late at all, John. Let's try a round. John! Be a sport! (*Cajoling.*) You can start.

JOHN (*Furious*). Just one game then, damn it! X!

DOROTHY (*Blows kiss to* JOHN). Y. (*To* ELLEN.) You're next. (*Pats sofa for* ELLEN *to side beside her.*)

ELLEN. . . . Z. . . .

CASS. XYZ? I challenge.

ELLEN. . . . I don't know . . . It just seemed to come after XY . . .

DOROTHY. John loves to start with X. The word was xylophone, wasn't it, dear. It usually is. (*To* ELLEN.) Now you're a third of a ghost.

ELLEN. I'm really so bad at games. (*Sits beside* DOROTHY.)

CASS (*Sits on chair near them*). Why don't we try something else? How about going around and starting a word with the last letter of the word before?

DOROTHY. Splendid! I like that one!

JOHN. Dorothy, I think we should go home.

DOROTHY. We haven't played one game yet, dear.

JOHN (*Angry*). All right, then, but *only one*. I'll start. Mountain.

73

DOROTHY. Never.

ELLEN. . . . Red?

CASS. Darling.

JOHN. Groan.

DOROTHY. Groan? . . . Gnome.

JOHN (*Righteous*). You're out. That word starts with a "g."

DOROTHY. Nome, Alaska doesn't.

JOHN. No proper names or place names. You're out. I start.

CASS. Do you always start no matter who—

DOROTHY. Isn't he dreadful? He's discovered that he can get away with it, so he does.

JOHN (*Scowling at* DOROTHY). Alternately.

DOROTHY (*To* ELLEN). I'm out.

ELLEN. Alternately . . . yellow?

CASS. Very good, honeybun. Wither.

JOHN. Reply . . .

ELLEN. . . . Yellow?

JOHN (*Kind*). Sorry, but you can't use the same word twice. You're out. I start.

CASS. Just the two of us?

JOHN. Stupid.

CASS. Diabolic.

JOHN. You're out. The word is diabolical.

CASS. (*Jumps to his feet*). Is there a dictionary—

JOHN. No, there isn't. I won.

DOROTHY (*Warning*). John—

CASS (*Verging on belligerent*). I'd like to try again.

JOHN (*Verging on contemptuous, sits*). All right. Let's step it up. I start. Clod.

CASS. Devil.

JOHN (*Faster*). Lunatic.

CASS. Catastrophic.

JOHN. Climax.

CASS. Xylophone.

JOHN (*Triumphant*). You're out. I win! You used a word that's been used before—

CASS. That was in another game—

JOHN. You're out.

DOROTHY (*Standing*). John, I'm afraid it's later than I thought.

CASS. Just a minute, Cleves, there's no rule anywhere that says you can't use a word from a previous game.

DOROTHY. John . . . !

JOHN. All right. . . . I start. Zahmahdah.

CASS. Zahmahdah. I challenge. There is no such word.

JOHN (*Very cool*). Arabic. Means "you are a welcome guest in my house." I win.

ELLEN. Arabic?

CASS. Who knows Arabic?

DOROTHY. John, really . . .

JOHN. Does anyone here speak Arabic?

(*There is a silence.*)

(*Stands.*) I win. Let's go home.

CASS (*Furious, crosses to* JOHN). Look here, Cleves, you may get away with that sort of thing in your own social set, but in the Akron Athletic Club you'd be *lynched.*

JOHN. Are you by any chance suggesting—

CASS. I'm not *suggesting.* I'm spelling it out for you. (*Clenches fist.*) And I'd be glad to add some punctuation— (*Slaps fist into palm.*) —to make it clearer.

JOHN. You try one comma and— (*Slaps fist in palm.*) period!

ELLEN (*Feverishly trying to make peace, starts clapping*). There's a game we play a lot in Akron. (JOHN *turns, glares at her.*) It goes like this. Do you know it? (*Hits her knees three times, then claps her hands, continues in steady rhythm.*)

DOROTHY (*Crosses to sofa and sits*). What a nice, bright girl you are! (*Tries to pick up the rhythm. Has some difficulty with it, but gradually gets it.*) That's jolly! Now what do we do?

ELLEN (*Both stop clapping for explanation of game*). On the clap you say the first thing that comes to your mind and you look at the next person as you say it. And he does the same thing.

(CASS *sits.*)

ELLEN. The first thing that comes to *his* mind after *your* word. If you lose the beat you're out.

DOROTHY. Couldn't be easier and we can *all* play. I suppose you two are *sharks*—

CASS. Ellen's played it more than I have. I don't really remember—

ELLEN. It's called Free Associations.

DOROTHY. Like a Rohrshach! Would you like to start, John?

JOHN (*Crosses to dining chair and sits, removed from them*). I don't want to play.

DOROTHY. All right, you needn't. *We'll* play. Let's begin.
(ELLEN, DOROTHY *and* CASS *are clapping out the beat. There is some difficulty getting started.* DOROTHY *is very giddy and gay.*)

CASS (*To* DOROTHY). You start.

DOROTHY. All right. Ready, everyone? . . . Man.

CASS. Woman.

ELLEN. Child.

DOROTHY. Nurse.

CASS. Sick.

77

ELLEN. Hospital.

DOROTHY. Ether.

CASS. Smell.

(JOHN *unconsciously taps out the beat unnoticed by them.*)

ELLEN. Bad.

DOROTHY. Good.

CASS (*To* JOHN). Rotten.

ELLEN (*Is thrown by last word*). Egg . . . oops . . . I missed the beat.

(JOHN *stands.*)

DOROTHY. I love it. (*All stop clapping.*) Now we play for real.

JOHN (*Moving chair into game*). I start.

(*There is one round of claps to establish the beat. Then they begin.*)

JOHN. Late.

DOROTHY. Night.

ELLEN. Police.

CASS. Crook.

JOHN. Man.

DOROTHY. Liar.

ELLEN. Cheat.

CASS. Husband.

JOHN. Master.

DOROTHY. Mistress.

ELLEN (*Reacts openly to* DOROTHY's *word and her word is slow in coming.* CASS *and* JOHN *lean in to note her reaction*). . . . Marry.

CASS. Ring.

JOHN. Wedding.

DOROTHY. Divorce.

ELLEN. Mistress. (*Gasps. Keeps clapping.*)

CASS. Guilt.

JOHN (*Winces, keeps clapping*). Blackmail.

DOROTHY (*To* JOHN). Secrets.

ELLEN. Kept. (*Winces.*)

CASS. Trouble.

JOHN. Help.

DOROTHY (*Murmurs under her breath, still clapping*). Trouble.

ELLEN. Mistress—Help!

CASS. Save.

JOHN. Life.

DOROTHY. Marriage.

ELLEN. Children.

CASS. Mother.

JOHN. Church.

DOROTHY. Sin.

ELLEN. Hate.

CASS. Love.

JOHN. Sex. (*Winces.*)

DOROTHY. Fun.

ELLEN (*Stops clapping, direct response to* DOROTHY). NO!

CASS (*Same way, straight dialogue to* ELLEN). Yes.

ELLEN (*To* JOHN. *Not clapping*). NO—

JOHN (*To* ELLEN, *not clapping*). Why?

CASS. Yes . . . why?

ELLEN (*Suddenly aware of the others*). I don't know. . . . Are we still playing?

JOHN. OF COURSE! (*Claps. Is only one.*)

DOROTHY (*Stands*). No. . . . I think John's tired . . . (*Starts to gather her things.*)

(CASS *stands.*)

JOHN. Now let's not be poor sports, Dorothy. Can't stop in the middle of a game. Nobody's won yet.

DOROTHY. I'm afraid we've stayed too long . . . for Mrs. Henderson.

JOHN (*Stands. Crosses to door*). I can't agree, but if you insist.

CASS. Too bad you have to leave so early.

DOROTHY (*Crosses to door. To* CASS, *unable to look at* ELLEN). So nice meeting you. Perhaps we'll see each other the next time you're in town. Don't forget, the Aquarium is charming. Don't miss it. Good night. (*Exits.*)

CASS. Mr. Cleves, any time you want to try another game—

JOHN. You're out of your league, Henderson. (*To* ELLEN, *with meaning.*) Good night! (*Exits. Closes door.*)

CASS. Oh brother! That's some game, that is!

ELLEN (*Who has collapsed on sofa*). Somebody had to do something, the way you were carrying on. I'm tired. I want to be alone. Cass . . . I kept my bargain, you got to see him, now please go away!

CASS. Ellen, I feel responsible for you. I mean, look at the way you behave. Ever since we met. First you're through with him—then the balloons! Then you're through with him—

ELLEN. What I do is my—

CASS. Yeah, I know, it's your life and if you want to put your neck back in the noose, it's your neck—but I gotta at least try to stop you.

ELLEN. Why?

CASS. Well—because I like you, we're friends. Friends! We almost got married today.

ELLEN. You're sweet, Cass, but I'm quite able to take care of myself.

CASS. Maybe you can if it's something like going around the world alone, but not with that guy. You can't play his game any more than I can! We play according to the rules. Cleves breaks them all and makes his own! I thought all I had to do was come to New York and get in to see

81

him . . . You know that he told me to go ahead and tell
Dorothy? Yeah! While you two were in there. Called my
bluff. And he knew he could! Saw right through me. For
all my talk I could no more tell Mrs. Cleves what he's
been up to— Well, I couldn't. So he won. I just . . . gave
up . . .

ELLEN. Not noticeably.

(*Through the next speech,* ELLEN *rises with tray, crosses
to* CASS *who puts his glass on it.* CASS *crosses to chest and
gets glass from there, puts it on tray.*)

CASS. Aaaagh, you can't fight him on his own terms. That's
what I'm trying to tell you. But you know something else,
Ellen? I'm not the kind of guy who gives up! Why should
I give up? *I'm* right and he's wrong! There are laws to protect people—the Bill of Rights—the Constitution—

(ELLEN *exits to kitchen.*)

I'll sue him, that's what I'll do! Right up to the Supreme
Court. I'll take him to the *Better Business Bureau!!!*

ELLEN (*Re-enters,* CASS *hands her two glasses*). What a marvelous idea—

CASS. That's the answer! I'm no eagle—

ELLEN (*Starting for kitchen*). No you're not, but they're very
scarce. (*Exits.*)

CASS. I don't want to be an eagle!

(ELLEN *re-enters.* CASS *hands her two more glasses. She
exits.*) And that's no sour grapes! I'd rather be down here
with the rest of the people, with normal, human instincts
and emotions, able to love, living within the law—

ELLEN (*Re-enters*). He's no criminal.

CASS. That's only because he's got a good lawyer.

ELLEN. —And he's no monster! He's a human being with instincts and emotions and he can love. He loves me. And from what you told me this afternoon about your life in Akron, you don't know much about love.

CASS. I'm full of love. It's all here— (*Thumping chest.*) —just waiting for the right person! It takes two! (*Helping* ELLEN *to straighten furniture.*) Oh, he'll keep taking as long as you keep giving, but he ain't giving nothing, honey, and I don't mean diamond necklaces.

ELLEN. Will you get out of here and leave me alone! John's coming back!

CASS. NO! It's too much of a waste, all your sweetness and love going to that bastard. (CASS *takes her by the arm and seats her.*) Sit down. Your grass appreciates it more than he does—putting your children into books instead of into bed! This is a nest? What's a nest without a mate? You think you've got a visiting eagle? You've got a dirty old cuckoo bird—got his own nest—you bet he has, patting his wife's ass like that—

ELLEN. He did not!

CASS. Not in front of you, but I caught him. And he's still gotta go around stealing other people's eggs. EGGS! Why you haven't even got an egg to sit on! You can't win with him, but you're so goddamn hung-up—you want to know what your hang-up is? Do you? You're a thirty-year-old child! You only *want* what you can't *have*.

83

(*The door opens, and* JOHN *enters.*)

That was quick.

JOHN. Oh? So you're still here!

CASS. Yes, I am, and I've got something to say.

JOHN. Don't bother. You may have—

CASS. Oh no, now you listen to me—

JOHN. I was about to say you may have everything you want.
Henderson, your plant will stay open, and you'll have sole
control of management. . . . Isn't that clear enough?

CASS. I don't understand. . . . What about the 607?

JOHN. In this case, I choose to ignore it . . . My God, man, you
are pounding on an open door. I am giving you exactly
what you've been shouting about.

CASS. Why?

JOHN. To get you the hell out of here!

CASS. You . . . your word doesn't mean anything—I want it in
writing.

JOHN. Very well. My attorney will take care of it. The papers
will be ready for you to sign next week. (*Crosses to* ELLEN.)
Now why don't you be a good fellow and leave us alone?

ELLEN. Cass, he'll keep his word.

CASS. Oh! You're a great authority on his promises, aren't you?

JOHN. A deal is a deal. Stop being a bore, man!

CASS (*Starting for bedroom*). I hate to think I've been boring
you.

JOHN. Now where's he going?

CASS (*Exiting to bedroom*). To get my suitcase.

(ELLEN *starts after him.*)

(CASS *re-enters.*) I'll be in your office next week. You'd better have that paper ready.

ELLEN. Cass—

CASS (*At door with suitcase, raincoat, and hat*). What I said to you just now—

ELLEN. It's not true.

CASS. Even if you win . . . you lose. (*Exits.*)

JOHN (*Takes off jacket*). Stubborn, slow-witted, churlish dolt of an adolescent and a sore winner to boot!

ELLEN. You won't . . . you wouldn't do anything to—

JOHN. Why are you so worried about him?

ELLEN. I suppose it's difficult for you to understand under the circumstances . . . but he's really a nice person.

JOHN (*Loosening tie*). Amateur. Nice persons don't belong in business. But let's forget about him. . . . I'm here and everything's all right again.

ELLEN. You sent Dorothy home?

JOHN. Of course.

ELLEN. She didn't mind?

JOHN. Why should she mind? Never said a word.

ELLEN. In the game—

JOHN. We might as well have played Russian Roulette. (*Tosses tie on sofa.*)

ELLEN. You don't think she . . . I couldn't help it—that awful word kept popping out—

JOHN. Nothing like that would ever occur to Dorothy. When you're married twenty years—

ELLEN. Yes, that was a revelation to me. After twenty years— sex is fun.

JOHN. Pet, try to understand.

ELLEN. I can't. I never dreamed—

JOHN. You never asked me.

ELLEN (*Incredulous*). Ask my lover if he sleeps with his wife? What is that? A little friendly pillow talk?

JOHN. It doesn't happen often.

ELLEN. But it happens. That's the shocker. How can you possibly sleep with one woman when you're supposedly in love with another? (*Wry.*) It's easy.

JOHN. . . . It's for the children.

ELLEN. They like to watch?

JOHN. It's only because of the children that Dorothy and I are still married, you know that. And since we must remain together and create a happy environment for them . . .

ELLEN. You mean like patting her . . . patting her.

JOHN. Now, pet, you're too big a person to let a little thing like that bother you. . . .

ELLEN. But why do you have to sleep with her?

JOHN. Because if I didn't—it just wouldn't be good for the children. Why must we talk about that? I'm here with you—

ELLEN. We do have to talk.

JOHN. —Where I want to be. With the most desirable woman in the world—the only woman I want—the one person who fills my thoughts day and night—

ELLEN. When you're not thinking about the horse and fighting with Cass and patting Dorothy—

JOHN. Ellen, I gave Henderson his way just now for only one reason. To get him out of our lives. Because I love you. At dinner, watching you trying to carry off that piece of insanity, I was furious with you, but at the same time you were so pathetic and adorable I wanted to take you in my arms right then and there and comfort you . . . And in this room . . . when you came back in this (*Touches her dress.*) . . . you do love me . . . we're a part of each other . . .

ELLEN. Yes, but now there are three of us.

JOHN (*Holds her*). Darling, I love you, that's all that matters. (*There is a pounding at the door and* CASS *bursts in, tries vainly to signal something.*)

CASS. Sweetheart, I'm back.

JOHN. What the *hell*—

CASS (*Overlapping*). A *husband* shouldn't leave his *wife* over a silly quarrel when it's all the *husband's* fault.

JOHN. What *is* this? More *blackmail?*

Act Two

(*In the confusion, the door opens and* DOROTHY *is there. Everything stops.*)

CASS. Well, I tried. . . .

(DOROTHY *looks at* CASS, *then* JOHN. JOHN *looks at* ELLEN, *then* DOROTHY.)

FAST CURTAIN

ACT TWO

Scene 2

PLACE: *The same.*

TIME: *Thursday morning, a week later.*

AT RISE: *The living room looks neat and somehow bare as most of the bric a brac has disappeared. In one corner are several large cartons, securely tied, as well as some empty ones neatly stacked. The table is set for breakfast for two.*

JOHN *enters from the bedroom, crosses to the door, opens it, and picks up the* TIMES. *He is freshly-showered, dressed for the office.*

JOHN. Ellen? Coffee ready?

ELLEN (*Off*). Coming right up.

JOHN (*Crossing to dining chair, sits*). I'm late again. I've been late every morning this week.

ELLEN (*Enters from kitchen with tray, two cups and saucers, and water heater. She is barefoot, wearing large, black-rimmed glasses, and dressed in a short, perk, cotton house-coat*). I'm sorry. I keep packing the coffee pot. Now I can't find it at all. I hope you don't mind instant. (*Puts powder into cups.*) Will our suite at the St. Regis have a proper kitchen?

JOHN. They have room service.

ELLEN (*Pouring water*). I hate to think of all my things going into storage. But it won't be for long. If only I can find a little white house we *both* like—

JOHN (*As* ELLEN *exits to kitchen with tray and warmer*). A house isn't anything to rush into. A week in this place and still no extra telephones. (*Calling.*) What did the telephone company say when you called them about the new lines?

ELLEN (*Enters*). They said: "Lady, how many times we have to tell you—Monday."

JOHN. Monday! This is only *Thursday!* I can't wait until Monday! I spent a weekend at the Athens Hilton and had extra lines and that was just for a couple of *days.*

ELLEN (*Packing carton*). What can you do? It's a monopoly. You know, I think all repairmen work a one-day week—Monday. It's a well-concealed trade secret . . . That's a joke. (JOHN *smiles weakly.*) Your back any better?

JOHN. No, I'm afraid it's not.

ELLEN. Poor John.

JOHN. I'm sorry. You must find it a dreary bore.

ELLEN. Oh, John! When you're in pain?

JOHN. It'll go away . . . some day. You're not being firm with those phone people—

ELLEN (*Crossing near him with carton*). I tried to be, but I guess I kept thinking we're moving anyway.

JOHN (*Noticing*). When did you start wearing glasses?

ELLEN. I got them yesterday. (*Flustered, as* JOHN *reaches for them, looks through them, then at her.*) They're deductible!

JOHN (*Giving them back*). Harold Lloyd didn't bother putting glass in his. Just as effective.

ELLEN (*Ingenuously*). I love the way you know about things like Harold Lloyd. Oh, there's still so much to do. (*Starts packing books from desk into carton on window seat.*) I went to my gynecologist yesterday, too, and he says I have a magnificent pelvis!

JOHN (*Buried in paper*). Isn't that nice.

ELLEN (*Taking books from shelf*). He says I can have a baby a year and drop them like peas out of a pod! (*Packing into carton.*) I'm built like a Chinese peasant!

JOHN (*Not listening*). You are?

ELLEN (*Beaming, takes more books from shelf*). Isn't that great?

JOHN. Great.

ELLEN (*Packing carton*). Let's make a baby right away!

JOHN (*Looks up from paper*). Dear, I have to go to the office—

ELLEN. I didn't mean this minute, silly. But as soon as your back is better? We don't have to wait until we're married to start one. You said Dorothy's going to Reno as soon as the agreement is signed.

JOHN. The lawyers are nowhere near—

ELLEN. We're losing time! We could just say it's a little premature! Lots of people do that—it's quite chic—

JOHN (*Kind but firm*). Dear, why don't you just finish your packing so the movers can get in here, hum?

(ELLEN *takes her coffee cup and crosses to desk.*)

ELLEN (*Quiet, chastened*). Must I take the wisteria off the ivy?

JOHN. No, you don't have to; but if you don't, someone else will have to. This *will* be the executive suite and cutesie touches are rather out of place.

ELLEN (*A pause*). Why didn't you ever tell me you thought they were cutesie?

JOHN. Let's just say they're inappropriate. . . . Come on now, don't look like that.

ELLEN. Please don't be cross with me.

JOHN. I'm not cross with you, am I?

ELLEN. . . . No . . .

JOHN. You know I've been deeply affected by losing Sweet Sam . . . and that, plus my back . . . and a general feeling of disorientation—

92

ELLEN (*Resumes packing books*). You poor baby. . . . You think you'll feel all right enough for tonight?

JOHN. What's tonight?

ELLEN. My dinner party at Pavillon. For my friends to meet you (JOHN *gazes at her impassively.*) Oh, I did forget to tell you, didn't I? Janice is coming in from Easthampton and Corky's back from the circus, and Joyce—she's reporting sick at her show, and . . . six of them. I've reserved a table for eight o'clock . . .

JOHN. It sounds enchanting, but you might have asked me if it would be convenient.

ELLEN. . . . I didn't know a wife had to ask.

JOHN. What if I had a meeting?

ELLEN. But you don't have meetings any more now that we . . . we're . . . Is it convenient?

JOHN. As convenient as it'll ever be. I've got to get down to the office.

ELLEN. Could I keep the Real Estate section?

JOHN. Yes—but Ellen, please, no more community club living —no matter how deluxe the development—in fact, no more developments! I must have room to breathe. (*Crossing to briefcase.*) Did you say eight o'clock?

ELLEN. John, do you still love me?

JOHN. Of course I still love you . . . I look forward to tonight. It'll be nice to eat out for a change. (*Quickly.*) A change for you.

ELLEN. You don't like my cooking—

JOHN. Like it! I love it! That okra casserole you made the other night with the cottage cheese and the poached egg was superb!

ELLEN. You hardly touched it!

JOHN. I've been off my feed lately with this damn heat . . . so much on my mind . . . now I must dash.

(*Buckles case.* ELLEN *runs to door and opens it.* JOHN *follows her.*)

You're not wearing shoes.

ELLEN. I never do if I can help it.

JOHN. Oh. I wasn't aware of it until recently.

ELLEN. You weren't around much until recently, remember? Like my housecoat?

JOHN. Very . . . suburban . . . (*Kisses her lightly.*) See you tonight. (*Exits.*)

ELLEN. Bye.

(ELLEN, *pensive, crosses to desk, gets pencil, crosses to table, gets paper, sits. There is a knock on the door.* ELLEN *crosses to door, opens it.* CASS *is in doorway with suitcase, raincoat, and a long white box.*)

ELLEN. Cass!

CASS. Hi.

ELLEN (*Delighted*). Cass! I never thought I'd see you again! Come in!

94

SCENE TWO

(CASS *enters, puts suitcase and coat down.*)

CASS (*Elaborately casual*). Just wanted to give you this—our product—fix that drawer of yours.

ELLEN (*Reading label*). "E-Z Pull Drawer Slides. Manufactured by the Henderson Machine and Tool Company, 321 Commerce Street, Akron, Ohio . . ."

CASS (*Pointing to fine print*). "The answer to the housewife's problem."

ELLEN. Wow.

(ELLEN *crosses to chest and puts box down, takes off glasses, and puts them on chest.*)

CASS (*Looking around*). You're moving.

ELLEN. Yes. This place isn't big enough for us.

CASS. For us. . . . Uh-huh.

ELLEN. Dorothy's going to Reno.

CASS. Well . . . congratulations.

ELLEN. Thank you.

CASS. So what else is new?

ELLEN. My whole life. I'm terribly happy.

CASS. Well . . . I guess you are . . . marriage plans always perk you up . . . I should really buy you a drink to celebrate, but it's kind of early—

ELLEN. It's never too early for champagne . . . remember?

CASS. Do you want me to—

ELLEN (*Exiting to kitchen*). Oh, no. I'm the lady of the house. (CASS *goes to chest, picks up* ELLEN's *glasses, tests them, puts them on.*)

(*Off.*) We've had dinner home every night this week, and John just loves my cooking. Cass, it's marvelous being together all the time. (*Re-enters.*) And it's such a *relief* to be going *straight*. (*She has brought a bottle and two glasses.*)

CASS (*Takes off glasses and hands them to* ELLEN). These help your eyes? (*Opening champagne.*)

ELLEN. Oh, enormously. (*Puts on glasses.*) Don't I look like a wife?

CASS (*Pouring champagne*). You sure do.

ELLEN. Dorothy's going to Reno.

CASS. You told me.

ELLEN. Oh. I did?

CASS (*Toasting*). Your future. I hope it's everything you hope.

ELLEN. Oh, it is, it is already and we haven't really begun our new life together. John can't wait to start a family.

CASS (*Accepting this*). You know, that night when I left here I was walking in circles. I must have been, because when I looked up I was right back in front of this house. I'm standing there in a fog when a cab pulls up, and it's Dorothy! All I could think of was I'd better get the hell back here before she did! Well . . . I tried . . . I really tried . . .

ELLEN. It was a good try.

CASS. What a night! Nothing like that ever happens in Akron. I was beginning to think I dreamed it. (*Looking into gar-*

den.) But no. There they are. Ellen, Ellen, how does your garden grow? Why, I buy them at the store and tie them on.

ELLEN. Cass, do you think they're cutesie?

CASS. What's cutesie?

ELLEN. Oh, you know, cutesie . . .

CASS. I think you're cutesie. I like that wrapper. You look real clean like that day you came out of the shower. And your glasses. You look great!

ELLEN. That's because I'm so happy.

CASS. Honey, I'm happy that you're happy.

ELLEN (*Turns from* CASS). I've never been so happy! Never. (*Voice breaks.* ELLEN *sinks on sofa.*) I never thought anyone could be this ha-happy—

CASS. What's the matter?

ELLEN (*Sobbing*). I know his back hurts . . . and he lost that damn horse. . . but—

CASS. He sure as hell wanted that horse.

ELLEN. He sure as hell wanted ME! Sometimes I think he doesn't even like me any more. We never make love. We used to stay up ALL NIGHT making lo—

CASS (*Sits beside her*). Maybe you should talk to him about that.

ELLEN. I *did*. He said that was *one* night a *week* and the next day . . . (CASS *takes glass from her hand.*) . . . he was like a *zombie*. But he doesn't even give me the one night I used to ha-have—

(CASS *takes her glasses off.*)

CASS (*Cuddles her*). Sex is a lot in the head, honeybun, and if he's got things on his mind—I mean, a guy's gotta be in the mood—

ELLEN. He's *always* in a mood—mopes around—hardly talks to me—comes home, has dinner, works on his papers—then he says he has to get some sleep, and before I can even say *goodnight* he's *snoring!*

CASS (*Patting her regularly*). You knew he snored—

ELLEN (*Sobbing*). How would I know? He never *slept!* I know it's a big adjustment for him—I know that—the morning papers and everything—

CASS. What's that got to do with—

ELLEN. Oh, he has all these habits—he used to read the papers on the train coming into New York in the morning—and now he's all mixed up and he doesn't know *when* to read them—and last night they were full of nail polish from when I did my toenails. I don't know why he got so mad, I didn't get any on the financial page—and he hates every little white house I find and whenever I mention our children he just freezes and when I told him how the doctor raved about my pelvis— (CASS *kisses her lightly.*) —he wasn't even *excited.*

(ELLEN *flops her head into* CASS's *lap, face upward.*)

CASS. You can drop 'em in the fields, can't you . . . I think that's just great.

ELLEN. He doesn't appreciate what a good pelvic measurement means to a woman.

CASS. No he doesn't honey.

ELLEN (*Puts her arm around his neck*). I've been so miserable and I couldn't tell anyone. Oh, Cass, I'm so glad to have you for a friend.

CASS. So am I, honey . . .

ELLEN. I feel so close to you.

CASS. Sure you do . . . (*Kisses her.*)

(ELLEN *breaks the kiss and sits up, pushing* CASS *away from her.*)

ELLEN (*Outraged*). Cass! I love John!

CASS. No, you don't. He's mean to you.

ELLEN. I do and he's not! The poor man's just—he's upset, that's all— (ELLEN *stands, puts on glasses, smoothes hair, straightens housecoat.*) Thank you for being so comforting.

CASS (*Rises*). Comforting?

ELLEN. Comforting.

CASS. *Comforting!*

ELLEN. *Comforting!* I'm sorry I slopped over . . . I—I've been unnerved . . . Let's just forget it. (*She takes up champagne bottle and starts to pour more, hostess voice.*) Here. It's delicious, isn't it?

(CASS *takes bottle away angrily and puts it down on coffee table.*)

99

(*Still the hostess.*) What brings you to New York this time?

CASS. You.

ELLEN. How's Betty?

CASS. Betty who?

ELLEN. Betty, that nice girl Betty you're going to marry. The one who works in your office—

CASS (*Explosively*). How do I know? I haven't looked at her all week! If I did I saw purple flowers and lawnmowers and diamond necklaces and balloons—

ELLEN. Cass! Please don't—

CASS. I may not be the right guy for you, but neither is that—

ELLEN. Please stop!

CASS. Okay, okay, the guy's got glamour, I'm willing to admit that. He's an important man—

ELLEN. —Attractive, charming, highly intelligent, amusing—

CASS. That depends on your point of view. All right, say he's all of those things. So are you. And besides you're lovable. There are thousands of guys around who could love you if you'd let them. Me, for instance. So I'm not such a big deal, I'm not glamorous, but I'm a *man* and I'd know how to love you and take care of you and be responsible for you which is more than anybody could say for John Cleves. If you marry him you don't need a baby—you've *got* one—

ELLEN. John is like a boy. That's why I love him. It's going to be all right with us. It's got to work.

CASS. What if it doesn't? What about us?

(CASS *goes to* ELLEN, *takes her glasses off, starts to move to kiss her when there is a knock on the door and the door, not latched, swings open. They break apart.*)

Timing is everything.

DOROTHY (*Enters dressed in linen dress of shocking pink*). Oh dear, I've done it again. The door wasn't latched and I gave it just the tiniest push and . . . (*Sees* CASS.) Well, here we are again!

CASS. Hi there, Mrs. Cleves, how are you?

DOROTHY. It's nice to see you again, Mr. Henderson. And Mrs. —Oh, dear, it's so confusing . . .

CASS. I was just leaving.

DOROTHY. *Please* don't go on *my* account. (*To* ELLEN.) You said any time between eleven and three today . . . but I'm afraid I'm early.

ELLEN. Oh, no—not at all—

DOROTHY (*To* CASS). Must you? Not even a minute for a chat?

CASS (*Crossing to door*). Sorry. I've got to check in at the Commodore and then see your husband—uh— (*Looks from* DOROTHY *to* ELLEN.) —your husband. I wish I could stay here. It'd be a lot more fun. So long. (DOROTHY *turns to garden.* ELLEN *crosses to* CASS. CASS *gives* ELLEN *back her glasses.*) You don't know it, but you've got rose-colored glass in these. (*Takes suitcase and coat and exits.* ELLEN *closes door behind him, hesitates, then turns to* DOROTHY.)

ELLEN. Mrs. Cleves, I can't tell you how sorry I am.

ACT Two

DOROTHY. None of that. Am I keeping you from something? Because if you're busy, I'll run over to Maximilian and fit my coat—wasn't that dear of John—his bon voyage gift— I can stop back here later—

ELLEN. No, no. I'm not doing a thing. Won't you sit down?

(DOROTHY *crosses to chair and sits, fusses with dress.*)

(ELLEN *crosses to sofa and sits. They eye each other covertly.*)

What a lovely dress.

DOROTHY. Isn't it? Adore the color. After so many years of dressing to please a man who thinks there's no color but black. Miss Gordon—

ELLEN. Ellen.

DOROTHY. Yes. Ellen. I hope you and I—

ELLEN. I would like us to be.

DOROTHY. There's no reason why we shouldn't—

ELLEN. —So much better for the children—I don't want them to be hurt.

DOROTHY. Of course.

ELLEN. How are they?

DOROTHY. Splendid. John wants to break the news to them himself, so I've told them he's out of town on business.

ELLEN (*Indicating the bottle*). Would you like some champagne?

DOROTHY. What a lovely idea!

ELLEN (*On her way to the kitchen*). I'm nervous about meeting them. I hope they'll like me. (*Exits.*)

DOROTHY. My dear, they like anything pretty, even poison oak. (*Regrets having said that, as* ELLEN *re-enters with glass wrapped in tissue paper.*) Now, did John tell you about the house? Well, traditionally I get it. But I think he should have it, and he said he'd talk to you about it.

ELLEN (*Crosses to sofa, sits, unwraps glass*). No, we haven't discussed it yet.

DOROTHY. Don't you think it would be better for you and John to live out there?

ELLEN. I don't know, really . . . I suppose it would give the children a sense of security when they visit us . . . and they'd have their own rooms to go back to. But where would *you* go?

DOROTHY. I hadn't really thought. I won't be around much. I'll be larking a good deal. Haven't been anywhere in ages. Jamaica, Hong Kong, Seville at Easter—might pop back early in May, then London in June—

ELLEN (*Pouring*). It sounds wonderful.

DOROTHY. I imagine when I get back from Reno I'll do some house hunting . . . (*Rises, crosses to coffee table to get glass.*) Actually, all I need is a little pied-à-terre. A place to keep my clothes. I'd been thinking about a hotel suite, but when I mentioned it to John, he was livid—not deductible, you know.

ELLEN (*Inspired*). Why don't you take this place? *Seriously.* The present tenant is moving out, it's owned by the company and therefore it's—

TOGETHER (DOROTHY *sits beside* ELLEN). —Tax-deductible.

DOROTHY. I love it. It's a marvelous idea! I love it. I *love* it! And John can't possibly say no because—

ELLEN (*As they clink glasses*). —That's right!

DOROTHY. Brilliant! I couldn't be more delighted! You must give me all the necessary information about this flat. (*Gets out notebook.*) I was so sure you'd agree about the house that I've made a list for you. We might as well get right down to it. (*Puts her glasses on.*)

I am *so* pleased about this place! (*Reads.*) Menus. Mrs. Jennings has them all—she's the housekeeper, her husband's the chauffeur—and my dear, hang on to them—they're accustomed to John and impossible to replace. She knows exactly what John wants for family dinners and entertaining. You'll be entertaining John's business associates and their wives three nights a week and most weekends. The staff gets Wednesday off because that is the one day John is out of town on business. (*Voice trails off, sips champagne, refers to notebook.*)

Drunk. Drunk? Oh, yes, if Mrs. Jennings seems drunk, she *is* drunk—particularly in the winter, but it's all so Wuthering Heights one can't blame her—as a matter of fact, if she appears the *least* bit out of sorts I suggest you present her with a bottle of brandy. She prefers Courvoisier. Gardens. Eric is the most superb gardener in Essex County. Just give him his head and constant praise. He's a gem. And there *are* ways of handling Ingrid—she's his wife. During the day, she's a stout prosaic woman in a housedress, but at night pure pagan—tears off her clothes and wanders around the grounds. I don't know why, but she's attracted to our terrace like some great, white moth, usually along with the demi-tasse. When someone notices her, as they inevitably do, I try to pass her off as a marble relic! (*She checks list.*) Now, the tennis courts—Jennings is quite good with them and actually enjoys—

ELLEN. Mrs. Cleves—

DOROTHY. Dorothy.

ELLEN. Dorothy. About Mrs. Jennings—I like to cook.

DOROTHY. It is most definitely one of the creative arts. God knows Mrs. Jennings has the temperament of a van Gogh.

ELLEN. Must there be a Mrs. Jennings?

DOROTHY. You're not—you couldn't be—no, you're not thinking of cooking for the staff yourself—on all that restaurant equipment—

ELLEN. Must there be a staff?

DOROTHY. With thirty-seven rooms and a wine cellar, yes. And lucky to have them.

ELLEN. It's not the way I've always thought of being married.

DOROTHY. I'm afraid you'll have to change your concept. (*Stands, business with gloves.*) It's the only way to be married to John.

ELLEN. Thirty-seven rooms . . . and I've been dreaming of a little white cottage and baking brownies— Oh, a cottage large enough for Johnny and Debby to have their own rooms and a place for their toys—

DOROTHY. Didn't John tell you about them?

105

ELLEN. We talked about them a lot.

DOROTHY. Really? Then he must have been a little vague. He *is* vague about them, you know, sees them so rarely. You see, Johnny's at Harvard, and Debby's at Bryn Mawr, my alma mater.

ELLEN. I didn't know. I thought they were younger. I mean a lot younger. (*Gestures to indicate toddlers.*)

(JOHN *bursts in with briefcase.*)

John!

DOROTHY. Surprise!

JOHN. Oh, you're all here. I'm going to get Sweet Sam and for less than a million. I'm catching the next plane. Oh, Dear . . .

ELLEN and DOROTHY (*Both answer*). Yes?

DOROTHY. Sorry.

JOHN. Ellen, pack my bag, will you? I'm in a tearing hurry. (ELLEN *starts for bedroom.*)

ELLEN. Which one? What'll I put in it?

JOHN (*Waving her to bedroom*). The small one. I may have to stay over. You know, shirt, shorts, socks, handkerchiefs, shaving things, you know—

(ELLEN *overhears first line of* DOROTHY's *and exits.*)

DOROTHY. John, could you give me just a moment? I was going to stop at the office on the way to fit my coat, but since you have to catch a plane—

JOHN. Of course. I like that dress.

DOROTHY. You do?

JOHN. I've always liked colors, and that's so, so vibrant. And so are you.

DOROTHY. I just got a whole new make-up. Maybe that's it.

JOHN. Whatever it is, you're positively blooming!

DOROTHY. Why, John! (*Flustered, crossing to sofa and sitting.*) John, if you could make it back tonight, I'd coerce the children into having dinner with us. And we could tell them about the divorce at the same time.

JOHN. If I can possibly be here, I will.

DOROTHY. If you're not back tonight, will you see them tomorrow?

JOHN. Absolutely. First thing on my agenda.

DOROTHY. Now, if you'll just sign the divorce papers.

JOHN. Darling. . . . Don't you think we're being a little hasty?

DOROTHY. No. They were drawn to everyone's satisfaction three days ago. I've made a reservation at a ranch. I want to get it over with.

JOHN (*Crosses to sofa and sits beside her*). Dorothy, you're behaving magnificently.

DOROTHY. Nonsense.

JOHN. I wonder if you have any idea how painful this is for me. When we met last Friday in Pete Mitchell's office . . . you and I across a table . . . all those filthy legal terms . . . the end of a life together.

DOROTHY. I know, I know. When we discussed the mausoleum —I'd always thought of us side by side, you and I and Johnny and Debby . . .

JOHN. You make it sound like a bus ride. It's a very serious thing.

DOROTHY. Of course it is, dear.

JOHN. It's very unsettling. My whole family together in my family's mausoleum and me rattling away somewhere by myself—

DOROTHY. You won't be alone, John. You'll be with Ellen.

JOHN. Ellen'll probably want to be with her own people. You always want to be with your own people.

DOROTHY. Maybe you could invite Ellen to be with us. That way we'd all be in one place.

JOHN (*Laughing at her and with her*). That's very thoughtful of you. But don't you think it's a little unseemly for me to lie in rest surrounded by wives?

DOROTHY. New England cemeteries are full of that sort of thing.

JOHN. Darling— (*Puts his hand on her thigh.*) — let's not do anything impulsive. Why don't we try a separation? Legal, of course. You'd be free, I'd be free. And we could still file a joint return.

DOROTHY (*Taking his hand from her thigh, and putting it on his own arm*). No, John. You can file a joint return with Ellen. Same thing.

JOHN. No, it's not . . . exactly . . . There are certain tax advantages to this arrangement—

Scene Two

DOROTHY. John, *we* are getting a divorce and *you* are marrying that poor girl! Really! (*A beat, then quizzical.*) Aren't you happy, John?

JOHN (*Uncomfortable*). That's a helluva thing to ask!

DOROTHY. Well, are you?

JOHN. I'm . . . disoriented. . . .

DOROTHY. Of course you are. But Ellen and I have arranged everything. Your life will go on exactly as it was. Except that Ellen will be there instead of me. Oh, you might give some thought to rigging up a little kitchen for her—the extra sewing room on the third floor might—

JOHN. Mrs. Jennings will do all the cooking, just as she always has.

DOROTHY. . . . And I'm taking *this* place.

JOHN. This is to be the executive suite.

DOROTHY. You've never had one! I think it's a *brilliant* idea, and to give credit where it's due, it was Ellen's. What a nice, bright girl she is. (*Almost flirtatious.*) Now, John, you're hardly in a position to fuss.

JOHN. It's too small! No place to entertain, no real comfort.

DOROTHY. I don't intend to entertain. I'm going to *be* entertained for a change. This place can be as comfortable as our upstairs sitting-room, and cosier because it's smaller. (*Seductive tones.*) John, I am *taking* this apartment!

JOHN. I've never seen you this way before! I like it!

DOROTHY. You do?

109

JOHN. Yes.

DOROTHY (*In retreat*). John, be nice to Ellen. She's better than you deserve, you rogue. (*Stands, business with gloves and purse.*) Remember, you promised to be with us tonight.

JOHN (*Crosses to her*). If I'm here, I certainly shall. Darling, about this place. . . .

DOROTHY. Not a word.

JOHN. All right. It's a typically devious female conspiracy— but all right. (*Close to her.*) Dorothy, I'm very fond of you. I'm going to miss you.

DOROTHY (*Takes gloves out, starts to put them on*). Just at first, until Ellen gets the hang of things. Tell her good-by for me, will you? John, I'm afraid I'll miss you.

JOHN (*Puts his hand on her arm*). Darling. . . .

DOROTHY (*Puts him off*). You're devastatingly attractive and you could charm a snake, but you're very poor husband material. Well— (*Crosses to door*) —I'm off to Maximilian's. (*Opens door.*)

JOHN (*Crosses to her*). Would you have dinner with me sometime?

DOROTHY. (*Amused*). Aren't you seductive! It's a delicious idea. Why not? When I'm here, and you're feeling like fun . . . call me . . . Any Wednesday. (*Exits.*)

JOHN (*Amused, then thoughtful, then after a moment*). Ellen! (*Crosses to coffee table and to desk looking for papers.*)

ELLEN (*Off*). Coming. (*Enters from bedroom, carrying over-*

night bag. She is clad in her Act One negligee and mules.)
Oh, Dorothy left. I wanted to say good-by.

JOHN. Yes, Dorothy left— (*Amazed to see her attire.*)

ELLEN. You didn't like me in the other one.

JOHN. I like you in anything, pet, but you did look as if you'd
just sent the children off to school in the car pool.

ELLEN. Suburban.

JOHN. I happen to feel that suburbia is as much of a blight as
billboards on country roads. (*Crosses to chest to look in
drawers.*) Dear, those papers I've been working on—
(*Business with briefcase.*) I wanted to read them on the
plane.

ELLEN. (*Delves into carton*). Maybe I packed them. (*Rum-
mages.*) Johnny must be very bright.

JOHN (*Searching in carton on window seat, starts to unpack
books and return them to bookcase*). Oh yes. So's Debby.

ELLEN (*Rummaging*). They must be the only college stu-
dents in the country with their little arms still flung over
their little heads . . . How old *are* they?

JOHN (*Putting a lot of books on shelf*). They're very precocious!

ELLEN. You know that conflict you had ever since you met
me? The one about going into their rooms at night to see
if they were covered? (*Crosses to him.*) That conflict?
Well, how did you ever get from Harvard to Bryn Mawr
and back to Short Hills in one night?

JOHN (*Putting more books on shelves*). Helicopter.

111

ELLEN (*Laughs in spite of herself*). John! You're shameless.

JOHN (*Laughing at himself*). I know it sounds ridiculous, but whenever I think of Johnny and Debby it's as if I hadn't seen them (*Gesture toward knees.*) for a long, long time.

ELLEN. And you don't want any more babies . . . You don't.

JOHN. I'll tell you about babies. Whenever I see one, I want to give it a cigar and discuss the Common Market.

ELLEN (*Accepts this*). John, you'll miss your plane.

JOHN (*Busily unpacking carton*). It's a shuttle service, they leave every hour.

ELLEN (*Watching him*). You know what you're doing? You're unpacking me. But that's all right. I didn't want thirty-seven rooms and a wine cellar and a staff and a husband who gives my babies cigars.

JOHN. Nonsense. Who was it that said marriage is a compromise?

ELLEN. Your wife.

JOHN. Really? I thought it was Thomas Jefferson. Well, anyway, we can have a white house and just bring the staff along. See how simple it is? Compromise.

ELLEN. Umhum . . . and what about Wednesdays?

JOHN (*Turns to another carton*). Wednesday will be just another day in the week.

ELLEN. You'll miss them.

JOHN. We'll have each other. (*Pulls out very rumpled papers from glass.*) Here they are. (*Tries to smooth them.*)

ELLEN (*Crosses to briefcase*). Oh John! I'm sorry.

JOHN. That's all right. I can still read them.

ELLEN. You're very patient with me.

JOHN. Of course. You're my child bride.

ELLEN (*Giving him briefcase*). I'm thirty years old.

JOHN (*Putting papers in case*). And still a child. Well, I'm off. My kingdom for a horse. . . . (*Pensive.*) I wonder if I'll still want Sam after I get him . . . You know how I am . . .

ELLEN (*A pause*). Yes, I know how you are . . .

JOHN. The last of the great ones, right?

ELLEN. Right.

(*Kisses her, takes overnight bag, and briefcase, crosses to door.* ELLEN *stands, crosses to him.*)

John, we've had some wonderful times together. I thank you.

JOHN (*A beat*). My pleasure. (*Opens door. Exits. Closes door.*)

(ELLEN *looks at closed door a moment, then crosses to closet, opens door, and slowly takes out balloons. She holds balloons a moment, then, making up her mind, crosses to terrace, lets balloons go, and watches them float out of sight. She crosses to phone and dials.*)

ELLEN. Information? I would like the number of the Commodore Hotel, East 42 Street. (*Listens.*) Thank you. (*Dials.*) I'd like to leave a message for Mr. Henderson—

Act Two

Mr. Cass Henderson. Just tell him I don't need balloons any more. *Balloons.* That's all. No name. He'll understand.

(*There is a knock on the door and* CASS *bursts in.*)

CASS. Ellen, I'm not the kind of guy who gives up.

ELLEN. Oh, Cass, I just called you—

CASS (*Exiting*). You want balloons? (*Re-enters with two enormous bunches of crazily shaped balloons.*) Here, balloons— (ELLEN *stares unbelievingly, then laughs as*)

FAST CURTAIN

114

F5